"Dr. Rosier gets it. She k̶ having lived it herself sin̶ lencies I could single out, ̶i̶n̶c̶l̶u̶d̶i̶n̶g̶ ̶t̶h̶e̶ ̶c̶l̶e̶a̶r̶ ̶a̶n̶d̶ ̶p̶u̶n̶g̶e̶n̶t̶ prose, I am most moved by the heart that infuses this memorable book of pithy and hard-earned advice. I will never forget the image of little Tamara sitting alone in the back seat of the family car after a set-to with her frazzled mom and whispering to herself the simple wish, 'I want a happy family.' Now grown up, Dr. Tamara Rosier proceeds to write a beautiful manual on how to make that wish come true."

Edward Hallowell, MD, author of
Driven to Distraction and *ADHD 2.0*

"Tamara knows ADHD personally, professionally, and academically, and her family has the stories to tell. In *You, Me, and Our ADHD Family*, she brings not only the strategies to make life at home easier but also tons of heart to help you feel like you aren't alone in this. She's the wise older sister you need in your life."

Ari Tuckman, PsyD, ADHD expert, author, and presenter

"As a follow-up to her excellent book *Your Brain's Not Broken*, Dr. Tamara Rosier's sequel, *You, Me, and Our ADHD Family*, could have been called *Your Family's Not Broken*. This volume takes on the complex topic of ADHD-affected family life. Dr. Rosier expertly guides readers through different relationship dynamics that will give them 'aha' experiences of finally being able to see and make sense of recurring, frustrating patterns. Dr. Rosier closes the deal with insightful and memorable ways to change these patterns from her rich experiences helping families, as well as with compassion drawn from her lived experiences."

J. Russell Ramsay, PhD, ABPP, author of *The Adult ADHD and Anxiety Workbook* and *Rethinking Adult ADHD*

"In her terrific new book, *You, Me, and Our ADHD Family*, ADHD coach, educator, and author Tamara Rosier manages the daunting task of helping you know that you aren't given a perfect family and that conflict, although unpleasant, is a natural part of human relationships. What to do when those disagreements arise, however, is where her expertise shines through. She offers you practical, effective tools for overcoming disputes and distance and nurturing self-awareness and connection instead. Using clear language to explain complicated information about the brain, emotions, and family systems, she leads you to understand how big feelings are contagious in families and relationships and what you can do to monitor and manage yourself more effectively. With thoughtful exercises designed to foster self-reflection, sample conversation techniques, real-life examples from clients, and key takeaways, she teaches you interventions to improve emotional regulation, empathy, distractedness, and broken attachments. Tamara courageously shares many lessons she has learned personally that add to the richness of this book. This is a must-read for anybody living in a neurodivergent family. I will be recommending it to my clients, my colleagues, and my friends."

Sharon Saline, PsyD, author of *What Your ADHD Child Wishes You Knew* and *The ADHD Solution Deck*

"Dr. Rosier has written an illuminating, insightful, and powerful book exploring the ways in which ADHD affects families. Her personal reflections and case studies are seamlessly woven into a practical framework along with invaluable advice for addressing the complex challenges of living with ADHD. At turns heartbreaking, humorous, reassuring, and direct, this is a must-read book on how to be a resilient ADHD family. I will recommend it to my patients and colleagues!"

Anthony L. Rostain, MD, MA, chair of the Department of Psychiatry and Behavioral Health, Cooper University Health Care

YOU, ME,
AND OUR
ADHD
FAMILY

YOU, ME,
AND OUR
ADHD
FAMILY

**PRACTICAL STEPS TO CULTIVATE
HEALTHY RELATIONSHIPS**

TAMARA ROSIER, PhD

Revell

a division of Baker Publishing Group
Grand Rapids, Michigan

Published by Revell
a division of Baker Publishing Group
Grand Rapids, Michigan
RevellBooks.com

Printed in the United States of America

Library of Congress Cataloging-in-Publication Data
Names: Rosier, Tamara, 1968– author.
Title: You, me, and our ADHD family : practical steps to cultivate healthy relationships / Tamara Rosier, PhD.
Other titles: You, me, and our Attention-deficit hyperactivity disorder family
Description: Grand Rapids, Michigan : Revell, a division of Baker Publishing Group, [2024] | Includes bibliographical references.
Identifiers: LCCN 2024001851 | ISBN 9780800745356 (paperback) | ISBN 9780800746445 (casebound) | ISBN 9781493447244 (ebook)
Subjects: LCSH: Attention-deficit hyperactivity disorder—Popular works. | People with attention-deficit hyperactivity disorder—Life skills guides. | Neurodivergent people—Life skills guides. | Attention-deficit disordered children—Life skills guides. | Families.
Classification: LCC RJ506.H9 R6655 2024 | DDC 618.92/8589—dc23/eng/20240424
LC record available at https://lccn.loc.gov/2024001851

This publication is intended to provide helpful and informative material on the subjects addressed. Readers should consult their personal health professionals before adopting any of the suggestions in this book or drawing inferences from it. The author and publisher expressly disclaim responsibility for any adverse effects arising from the use or application of the information contained in this book.

The names and details of the people and situations described in this book have been changed or presented in composite form in order to ensure the privacy of those with whom the author has worked.

Baker Publishing Group publications use paper produced from sustainable forestry practices and postconsumer waste whenever possible.

24 25 26 27 28 29 30   7 6 5 4 3 2 1

To my fabulous family. Your influence has shaped the person I am today and the words within these pages. Thank you for the countless lessons, the boundless love, and the indelible mark you've left on my heart.

CONTENTS

FOREWORD

From the minute I met Tamara at the International ADHD Conference in 2019, I knew we were destined to be fast friends and close colleagues. She was deep into an animated conversation with our mutual friend Ari Tuckman, and I could tell from her passion, her intelligence, and her big laugh that she was someone I needed to meet. When Tamara paused for a breath of air, Ari graciously introduced me. Tamara was fantastic—so interesting and so vibrant. I had no idea of how accomplished she was, the significant impact of her work on the ADHD community, and her respected leadership among coaches. I only knew that once we started chatting, we couldn't stop. In the span of fifteen minutes, our friendship was cemented. When she asked me to write a foreword for this book, I immediately and wholeheartedly agreed.

If you have ADHD, then you naturally come from (and may currently live with) a family touched by ADHD. You may feel close to siblings, parents, and extended family members who treat you with acceptance, humor, and compassion. Or perhaps you have chosen to distance yourself from those relatives who seem to hurt you more than they show support or love. Whatever your situation may be, living with ADHD in combination with your family

11

history has affected who you are, how you choose to show up in the world, and the complexity of your identity. In order to become the healthiest version of yourself and create satisfying work situations and personal relationships, you will have to find a balance for getting along with those closest to you. This insightful, empowering book offers you a road map for getting there.

Families are complex, and families living with neurodivergence present unique challenges for folks. When you're quick to get angry, blame, and say unkind things, it's tough to know how to change old patterns of conflict and disconnection into new ones of healthy empathy, effective communication, and meaningful repair. Tamara Rosier has been a successful coach, trainer, and educator for almost thirty years. Her experience, both professional and personal, is threaded throughout this book, bringing richness and revelation to readers in ways that are remarkably insightful, inspiring, and courageous. She gets vulnerable about the ups and downs of her own familial relationships and shares what has helped her, along with thousands of clients, make meaningful changes that foster cooperation, closeness, and healing.

In *You, Me, and Our ADHD Family*, Tamara manages the daunting task of helping you know that you aren't given a perfect family and that conflict is a natural part of being engaged in relationships. What to do when those disagreements arise, however, is where her expertise shines through. Using clear language to explain complicated information about the brain, emotions, and family systems, she leads you to understand how big feelings are contagious in families and what you can do to monitor and manage yourself more effectively. She deftly examines the differences between survival and transformational thinking so you can accept your struggles and strive toward change without shame or blame. After explaining how family members' nervous systems affect each other, she offers thoughtful tools to assist you in widening your window of tolerance, reducing reactivity, and gaining perspective by controlling your telephoto lens. She describes three types of empathy and poses concrete strategies for when and how to use them. She also clearly shows the differences between healthy and treacherous triangulation in families and how you can avoid the pitfalls that lead to intense arguments and toxic alliances.

The structure of this book is geared toward helping you reflect on your own memories, behavioral patterns, and interactions with others. With exercises designed to foster self-reflection, sample conversation techniques, real-life examples from clients, and key takeaways, she teaches you about interventions for common emotional errors, mischievous monkeys that distort your thinking, upregulation and downregulation hurdles, and communication quirks. I especially liked the concluding chapters on reaching, repairing, and reconnecting as Tamara describes how to overcome avoidance and shutdown in relationships, how to be appropriately accountable, how to make sincere amends, and how to rebuild broken attachments. Her own poignant path touched me deeply as I read through the text.

You, Me, and Our ADHD Family is a rare gem. Tamara really gets what it is like to live with and among ADHD, and when you read this book, you feel like she is talking directly to you with warmth and wisdom. The book demystifies the delicate balance between individuality and togetherness in families. It helps you realize that everybody needs to understand ADHD, learn how to manage it (or their relationship to it), and figure out how to focus *together* on pivoting and trying again when issues arise. This is not a quick fix but rather a determined, sometimes confusing journey. Luckily, Tamara Rosier has written a terrific book to accompany you along the way.

Sharon Saline, PsyD, author of *What Your ADHD Child Wishes You Knew* and *The ADHD Solution Deck*
DrSharonSaline.com

INTRODUCTION
What Matters Most

I watched from the back seat of the wood-paneled station wagon as a mother and her daughter walked together, laughing as they crossed the parking lot toward the grocery store. The girl, approximately my age, skipped joyfully alongside her mother, engaging in cheerful conversation. They looked relaxed and glad to be with each other.

Meanwhile, my mother and sister were in the store. Opting to stay in the car, I sat there with my face still hot and streaked from crying. It had been a difficult day. That morning, before school, my mother had unleashed a torrent of anger at me over something I couldn't quite decipher. I arrived at school upset, nauseated, and unable to concentrate. My teacher detained me during morning recess due to unfinished worksheets from the previous night. And now, in the car, I found myself still reeling from a scolding for having forgotten to lock the front door that morning. "Do you want someone to break in? What were you thinking?" my mother had shouted. Days like this left me feeling overwhelmed, angry, and lonely.

I traced my hand along the vinyl seat as I watched the girl outside playfully jumping on the rubber pad, activating the automatic doors as if by magic. "Ta-da!" she seemed to proclaim as she extended her arms theatrically. Her mother responded with laughter, and their happiness was evident.

In a whisper, I confessed to myself, "I want a happy family." I resolved that the family I created in the future would be significantly different from the one I now knew. I aspired to emulate the mother I observed in the parking lot—relaxed, joyful, and deeply connected with her child. At that time, my sentiments were encapsulated in a simple phrase: "I want a happy family." Now I understand that what I yearned for were nurturing, positive, and fulfilling relationships within my family. I had no idea how difficult that journey would be for me.

Family relationships are complex and multifaceted. Each person possesses both positive and negative aspects, which they might choose to conceal from the outside world but reveal to their family. As imperfect people come together to make a family, there is a dynamic mix of love, disagreements, and maintenance. A happy family requires a lot of work.

In retrospect, I believe my mother struggled with ADHD symptoms, and I have compassion for her challenging circumstances. As a young divorcée in the 1970s, she juggled full-time work while raising two girls. I appreciated her efforts to infuse our childhood with fun through weekend camping trips and various adventures. However, her lack of organizational skills, impulsiveness, and emotional turbulence left a lasting impact on me. My days lacked a predictable structure, characterized by inconsistent bedtimes, frequent fast food, and excessive television consumption. I was confounded by her inconsistency in disciplining me, alternating between punishment and permissiveness. Also confusing was her tendency to become overwhelmed and lash out over minor details. I often felt that our family was fundamentally different because we were just trying to get through our days. Back then, there was little understanding of ADHD or how it could affect a family. With hindsight, everything makes sense now.

The emotional impact of ADHD on relationships, communication, and organization permeates the entire family, adding layers of complexity and stress to the system. While our homes should ideally serve as sanctuaries where our deepest needs for love and security are met, these fundamental aspects get lost in the chaos of trying to manage daily events. Families with members who possess neurodivergent traits such as ADHD, autism, and dyslexia must discover ways to foster respect, love, and connection, even when their neurodiversity poses challenges.

When I became a mother, I frequently found myself disheartened and frustrated with my own shortcomings. My ADHD traits rendered my aspiration of having an easygoing, happy family an uphill battle. I was quickly overwhelmed by the minutiae of daily life, often shedding tears when I believed I was failing as a mother.

Sometimes I would try hard to show up as a good parent, but things still didn't go right. Like when I piled my three children—ages one, eight, and ten—into our minivan for a much-anticipated trip to a local amusement park, our very own "Walley World." I felt utterly drained as I sank into the front seat after packing the stroller, snacks, diaper bag, and water bottles. After an hour's drive, we finally arrived in the crowded parking lot, where bored-looking teens in fluorescent vests waved us into vacant spots. Relief washed over me, but it was short-lived. From the back seat came a nervous exclamation: "Uh-oh!"

I instinctively groaned.

My eight-year-old daughter piped up, "I forgot my shoes."

I wasn't angry at the shoeless kid; I was sad. My sadness stemmed from a profound sense of my inability to manage not only my life but also the lives of those dependent on me. If I could go back to that moment, I would tell the younger version of me four essential insights:

1. You have ADHD, which makes managing all this overwhelming and challenging.

2. Your barefoot daughter also has ADHD.

3. Don't fixate on the details of socks and shoes. Instead, focus on the core element—relationships.

4. How you navigate this situation and others will strengthen or weaken your bond with your children.

Ultimately, strong relationships are the basis of family life. This book is about what I learned along the way.

This book isn't just for parents, though. In fact, it's not a parenting manual at all. It is an exploration of how to cultivate and sustain healthy relationships within a neurodiverse family. It is written for the ADHD adult seeking emotional growth and enhanced family connections. It's for siblings desiring mature relationships with the same individuals who were their partners in childhood antics. It's an invitation that extends to grandparents, who are treasure troves of love and comfort, seeking to connect with their grandchildren. This book also reaches out to aunts, uncles, and cousins within neurodiverse families, offering diverse perspectives from outside the nuclear family.

The book unfolds in two parts. Part 1, "It Begins with You," prepares you for family interactions by asking you to learn about yourself, analyze your tendencies, and balance your emotions. Understanding yourself is paramount because while you cannot control or change your family members, you can manage your own responses and behavior in a healthy manner.

Chapter 1, "Welcome to the Goat Rodeo," delves into how ADHD affects families by examining everyday misadventures and holiday mishaps. This chapter serves as a springboard for you to reflect on your own family dynamics and the potential influence of ADHD.

Chapter 2, "Is It You, Me, or ADHD?," equips you to identify ADHD traits and their impact on relationships.

Chapter 3, "Monkey Malarky," encourages the imaginative portrayal of ADHD symptoms as monkeys and suggests naming them as such. Even if you are already familiar with your ADHD traits, exploring this metaphor may reveal nuanced aspects of their influence. For those without ADHD, it offers a glimpse into the internal dialogues of individuals with ADHD, shedding light on their seemingly mysterious behaviors.

Chapter 4, "Understanding the Story of Emotions," underscores the significance of emotions in everyone's lives, urging you to trace your secondary emotions back to your primary emotions to gain a deeper understanding of yourself.

Chapter 5, "Everyday Emotional Missteps," challenges you to recognize the emotional fallacies you may be ascribing to, ultimately guiding you toward healthier relationships by acknowledging your own missteps.

Chapters 6 and 7, "Your Nervous System Isn't Broken" and "Widening the Window," explore the functioning of the nervous system, emphasizing the ease with which it can become disturbed. They also provide insights into how to balance your nervous system, enabling you to remain composed even in challenging family situations.

Chapter 8, "Perils of the Telephoto Lens," introduces the concepts of survival thinking and transformational thinking, which are helpful to keep in mind as you progress through the book.

Chapter 9, "Safety First," challenges you to think about emotional safety and asks you the personally challenging question, "Are you a safe person for others?"

The first nine chapters equip you to become a positive influence within your family. Part 2, "Ready for the Rodeo," immerses you in the context of your family.

In chapters 10 and 11, "Scorpions, Skunks, and Pesky Peccadilloes" and "Peccadilloes and Preferences," you will learn to categorize your family's behaviors into various levels of problematic behaviors, a skill that will prove invaluable in addressing those issues.

Chapters 12 and 13, "Going for a Swim" and "Pool Rules," introduce the metaphor of a pool in which intense emotions like fear, anger, joy, sadness, disgust, and surprise reside. This pool serves as a tool for identifying and managing overwhelming emotions effectively, both for individuals and for their families.

Chapter 14, "Good Morning, Poison Squirrels," addresses the communication quirks that may occur in families affected by ADHD.

Chapter 15, "Monkey Chatter," delves into how powerful

emotions can permeate family environments, affecting everyone in their proximity. You will learn to identify and address these patterns.

Chapter 16, "Unregulated Empathy," discusses how many people with ADHD sometimes have too much empathy and other times have too little. We'll address the challenge of managing empathy.

Because conflict is inevitable, there are four chapters dedicated to it. In chapter 17, "Triangles," we look at relational triangles and how they may contribute to conflicts and emotional difficulties in your family. Chapters 18, 19, and 20, "ADHD-Fueled Disputes," "Deliberate Discussions," and "Reach, Repair, and Reconnect," are dedicated to guiding you in resolving disagreements constructively.

Chapter 21, "Relating," concludes that, amid the imperfections, the true essence of family lies in the enduring connections that withstand the tests of time.

Real families are far from the idyllic scenes portrayed in Hall-mark movies, where people living in Connecticut wear cozy sweaters and casually sip hot cocoa while chatting about their perfectly adorned Christmas tree. Real families are complex, occasionally stepping on each other's toes as they navigate the intricacies of life. We are all works in progress.

I am deeply thankful for my husband, my children, and their significant others, who have extended grace and love, allowing me to continue growing. While we have encountered numerous setbacks, we have diligently worked toward cultivating a family culture rooted in encouragement, kindness, and care. Despite our failures, we persevere in our growth.

Whether it's in our relationships with parents, siblings, or extended family members, robust familial bonds play an integral role in our overall well-being and personal development. These bonds are among the most valuable connections we possess in our lives. My earnest hope is that, even if your family tree doesn't resemble someone else's or it features a few broken branches, you will discover ways to interact with your loved ones in a healthy manner. It all begins with you.

PART ONE

IT BEGINS WITH YOU

1

WELCOME TO THE GOAT RODEO

Family relationships are probably the most intense, frustrating, fulfilling, intimate, and delightful relationships that we will ever have. They can be both a tremendous source of joy and one of our greatest stressors. Sometimes we rejoice in the sweet times of harmony and deep connection. But more times than not, we fall out of step with one another. Too often we attempt to be a "happy family," expecting to move seamlessly through communication snags and emotional hazards while remaining in constant step with one another. That's not realistic. And although we love each other, we can each get in the way of that love by acting selfishly, rudely, and even viciously. It's family, and it's complicated.

Meet Carly, Lily, Tara, and John and their not-so-thankful holiday. It began with a text between the sisters. "Are you going home for Thanksgiving?" Carly asked Lily.

Lily, a third-year law student, felt immediately overwhelmed by the question. Her mind raced. *It's a five-and-a-half-hour car ride home. My classes don't end until 3:00 p.m. Wednesday. Oh, and with the time zone difference driving home, I'll lose an hour.*

Once I pack my car, I wouldn't get there until late. I'd have to leave their house by 4:00 p.m. on Saturday so I can have a day in my apartment to prepare for the following week. Oh, and I have that paper due. When will I finish that? The cadence of her thoughts hastened. *Then I'd have to find someone to feed my cat, and my laundry would need to be done. Ugh, I'm already so behind on the laundry. What would I pack? When would I pack? Am I overdue for an oil change? Tires. Wasn't I supposed to do something about my car tires this past summer?* She felt overwhelmed with her speeding thoughts and texted Carly, "I just don't think I can do it."

Lily has ADHD, a neurodevelopmental disorder affecting a person's ability to manage one thought at a time, control impulses, and regulate behavior. People with ADHD often struggle with prioritizing tasks and assessing their importance, making it difficult to differentiate between tasks that require immediate attention and those that can be put off. As a result, they may struggle to complete tasks efficiently and effectively, leading to poor performance, low productivity, and difficulty in relationships. Additionally, they may have problems regulating their emotional responses to situations. Like Lily, they may become easily overwhelmed by minor stressors and perceive them as major threats. Sometimes those with ADHD concentrate on minor issues and lose sight of the more significant challenges that require attention.

Carly looked at her phone and gave an audible "ugh" when she read Lily's response. *Why won't she prioritize our family? She misses so many of our family events for no good reason,* she thought. She was hurt. Her sister's inability to organize and plan her life felt like a personal grudge against Carly. "K," she replied to the text.

ADHD adds significantly to the complexity of creating healthy family relationships. When a family member has ADHD, it can affect the whole family. Studies indicate that when at least one person in the family has ADHD, it can affect how satisfied parents, siblings, and others in the family feel with their everyday life.[1]

Tara, the siblings' mother, called Carly a day later. "I'm calling to go over plans for Thanksgiving. What time do you think you'll be at our house? And is Blake joining us?"

Carly answered that she and her boyfriend would probably roll into her parents' house around 5:00 p.m. on Wednesday. "I wish Lily was going to be there. I hate how she always misses our family events," Carly vented.

"What! She's not coming?" Tara exploded. "This is the first I've heard of it, for crying out loud! She better come home! She better figure it out! Geesh!"

Though shocked at the intensity of her mom's emotions, Carly added more complaints about her sister's inability to get her act together, stoking Tara's fire. Eventually, the conversation converged on their disapproval of Lily's life choices.

ADHD often runs in families, and most experts believe that the genes you get from your parents play a significant role in causing the condition. Studies indicate that if someone in your family has ADHD, it's more probable that your parents and siblings also have it.[2] This family assumed that although Tara had not been officially diagnosed with ADHD, she most likely had it. She became overwhelmed quickly, misplaced items frequently, and tended to have emotional outbursts.

Somehow, Lily got wind of the conversation between her mother and her sister and their complaints. She called her grandpa John and explained how she felt hurt. Talking to her grandpa was reassuring because he always seemed to understand her. Lily suspected that he, too, had ADHD but was undiagnosed. After hanging up, she felt better.

Grandpa John then called his daughter, Tara, to defend Lily. And that was when the Thanksgiving debacle of 2022 ignited.

That debacle wasn't an isolated incident for this close-knit quartet. Unless they make some changes, variations of this chaotic scenario may continue to unfold and repeat.

Destructive behaviors like triangulation, boundary violations, and attempts to reshape others pose a significant threat to familial peace. In this book, you will discover strategies to maintain your equilibrium and avoid being drawn into the whirlpool of family strife. Additionally, you'll acquire valuable insights into cultivating more nurturing and harmonious relationships.

Perhaps you've found yourself drawn to this book because you're navigating family dynamics that feel like a chaotic goat rodeo. (I'm not entirely sure what a goat rodeo entails, but chaos seems like a fair bet.) You might be wrestling with the belief that your family is an absolute mess and you have no options but to resign and watch the impending bedlam unfold. Or it might not be that dire, but the people you hold dear have a knack for pushing your buttons and driving you up the wall. Or, sadly, your family might have inflicted deep wounds, and you're searching for a path toward healing and moving forward. At some point, we've all been caught in the tumultuousness of family dynamics, akin to a rodeo rider fighting to maintain his grip. Our entire focus narrows to the struggle to stay on while the horse bucks, twists, and kicks with all its might, determined to unseat its rider.

The Daily Rodeo

For some of you, it's not about the extraordinary rodeo spectacle; it's more like the everyday rodeo of family life. Instead of the chaotic goat rodeo, you're immersed in the daily juggling act that comes with family responsibilities. Rather than trying to wrangle a steer to the ground, you spend your mornings struggling to coax your child out of bed. Your version of a bareback bronco ride occurs during your son's meltdowns, where you cling to your sanity until the show is over. And then there's the barrel-racing competition, but in this rodeo, it's not a horse and rider navigating a cloverleaf pattern around barrels; it's you racing between football practice, gymnastics, Boy Scouts, and school events like a true rodeo champion.

One young couple joined me on separate computers in a Zoom meeting—Zach from work and Mina from their home. "We're hoping you can help us with our son, Trevor," Mina said. "He has ADHD." Their faces were peering at me from the little boxes on my screen, tense and desperate. I've seen that look before. It's the how-can-I-love-my-kid-so-much-and-hate-him-so-much-at-the-same-time look. And sometimes it's followed by the please-help-because-we-are-losing-our-darn-minds look.

"He really has a tough time with his emotions, and he always flips his lid," Mina said.

"I dread trying to get him to do anything," Zach confessed, his frustration evident in his voice. "I'll say, 'Let's go, buddy,' and he somehow hears, 'Go find that missing LEGO piece, give your bearded dragon two crickets, and change your shoes.' I have to tell you, I finally lost it yesterday and yelled at him."

Mina nodded in agreement. "Yeah, it's been really tough."

Mina and Zach told me about their experiences, candidly portraying their day-to-day rodeo challenges with Trevor getting out of bed, having breakfast, and departing for school. The confrontations unfolded like a predictable script, involving a series of persuasions and enticements and inevitably escalating to shouts, leaving everyone seething with frustration. They found themselves living out a situation that aligns with established research findings: Families with ADHD present often encounter persistently fewer positive interactions, resulting in an atmosphere of discontent at home characterized by high negativity and conflict.[3]

Zach and Mina had already recognized that punitive measures weren't effective in modifying their son's behavior. Instead, they designed a reward system. Trevor earned a token each time he did something right. He received a token if he promptly brushed his teeth after a single reminder. If he politely asked his sister for his toy, another token was in the offing. Their strategy was simple: catch him doing something right. It was a sound approach, except for one catch—it wasn't proving as motivating for Trevor anymore. Like many other children with ADHD, his enthusiasm for earning tokens had waned, rendering the rewards less influential in shaping his behavior.

"And to make matters worse," Zach added, "Mina and I fight about how to manage Trevor and the other two kids. We are all stressed."

The relentless demands children with ADHD place on parents' time and attention can stretch family bonds to their limits, leading to strained relationships, diminished quality time together, and an increase in conflicts. Research indicates that parents raising children with ADHD face higher divorce rates and a heightened risk of experiencing depression when compared to their counterparts in other families.

"Who else in your family has ADHD?" I asked. Understanding who shared ADHD tendencies was important as we examined family dynamics.

Zach responded first. "I was diagnosed as a child. And I just started treating it with medication a year ago."

Mina added, "I haven't been diagnosed officially, but I think I have it too."

If both parents have ADHD, the likelihood of their children having it is very high. Zach and Mina's house was filled with individuals with ADHD, but they hadn't accounted for that. Every person in their home needed to understand their ADHD, learn to manage it, and then determine ways of working together.

Many parents seek my guidance to address their child's challenges. Yet it's essential to recognize that they're part of a family. Instead of zeroing in on an individual, let's shift our focus to the family unit.

I encouraged Zach and Mina to explore how ADHD affects their family and discover new approaches to working together effectively. They applied many of the strategies from this book, like monkey talk (chapter 3) and the pool metaphor (chapters 12 and 13) as they worked as a family to address their ADHD together.

Your Family Tree

"I never realized that you and Dad were so young when you had me. You guys were still figuring out life," my twenty-seven-year-old daughter said recently. (She's the shoeless one from the introduction who grew up to be a great adult.) "I mean, you were my age when you had two kids. I can't imagine being a parent at my age." She now realizes that as she was growing up, she was also in the midst of other people who were still growing up. Fortunately, my daughter's insight comes with compassion.

Each person in your family is on their own journey to finding selfhood and significance—and it takes a lifetime of work to accomplish. Even the older folks who have been around your entire life are still figuring it out.

Families are a bunch of individuals, sometimes related by blood and sometimes not, who are all trying their best to make sense of their lives. When you are in a family, you see each other in your most vulnerable, angry, expressive, and heartbroken moments. You share the same spaces—bedrooms, kitchen tables, living rooms, backyards, and back seats. In a family is where you learn to test boundaries and push buttons with precision and accuracy. It is where you practice the craft of arguing and defending. It is where you pick up your first identity of cowboy, judge, triple crown winner, hazer, or rodeo clown. And hopefully, it is where you learn to apologize and forgive. But through it all, you are impacted by the experience, and you create the enduring bond of shared history.

Clients often ask, "Who exactly counts as my family?" They ask this because their current situation extends beyond the definition of a family as a group of two or more persons related by birth, marriage, or adoption who live together. Families look different for many of us. They include the relationships with people we have bonded with over years and who have seen the real, unpolished version of us. In addition to my husband and children, seventy-eight-year-old Phyllis, who was a friend of my aunt, is a big part of my life. I can't imagine holidays without Aunt Phyllis because she has been a facet in my life since I was seven years old. She's my family. Who is your family?

Don't worry if your family tree looks a bit wonky. I haven't met anyone without a few blemishes on their tree. Perhaps your aunt doesn't appreciate personal boundaries and asks about your dating life in the middle of a family dinner. Or your brother never really grew up and is still living in your parents' basement. Or your great-uncle has PTSD from the war that no one can speak of. It might even be more severe and closer to home, like emotional abuse, alcoholism, or drug addiction. Everyone, it seems, has some level of dysfunction in their family.

This book focuses on how families with ADHD can develop healthy relationships. Once family members understand how to maintain healthy relationships, the rest falls into place. So whoever you are in your family—parent, adult child, sibling, or the aunt who only visits for holidays—I invite you to discover how to remain emotionally healthy while being in your family.

The first part of this book concentrates on helping you formulate the most steadied and centered version of you possible. We'll look at what it is about ADHD that contributes to disorder in the family, identify your specific ADHD symptoms and how they affect you, and discuss avoiding emotional errors. Then we'll examine how you can find balance within yourself so you can become un-mess-with-able, meaning you are not easily goaded into emotional errors and survival thinking.

Before you begin a book like this, it's good to prepare yourself:

- Are you willing to be curious about what you can do to make your family experience better? Curiosity isn't quick to judge. When someone is curious, they are relaxed and ask questions.
- Are you willing to be aware of your own emotional state as you read? Write down your thoughts and feelings when

you read something that makes you angry or sad. Think about why you feel that way.

- Are you willing to focus on yourself? Trying to change others, although incredibly tempting and often preferable, isn't wise. The real growth comes from your willingness to change yourself.

Taking time to think about these questions is important because creating a healthy family begins with you.

2

IS IT YOU, ME, OR ADHD?

Vincent and K. C. were stuck in a rut. They knew they loved each other deeply, but living together was starting to feel like a chore. Petty arguments about everyday tasks drove them apart, and their relationship was far from what it used to be. They were once adventurous and enjoyed outdoor activities. They could still remember their most meaningful conversations from the early days of their relationship, which took place while they prepared to sail or wandered through the woods. Despite their current struggles, they still treasured their friendship and romantic bond. But it felt like their relationship might slip away if they didn't find a way to rekindle their connection.

Before we start to repair their relationship, it's helpful to understand how ADHD is impacting it. Relationship conflicts are frequently rooted in underlying factors such as working memory difficulties and emotional dysregulation. In this chapter, we'll explore various ways these issues can manifest. As we look closer at the relationship between K. C. and Vincent, remember that these patterns are not unique to just married couples; you might observe similar trends within your own family.

Working Memory Glitches

"My brain is always dashing from one thing to another," Vincent shared. "I feel like I am always playing catch-up. K. C. doesn't get it. When I come home after work, I am overwhelmed and exhausted. I don't want to do housework or help with the kids; I just want to crawl into a cave. I just need the world to stop for a minute."

It's hard for those without ADHD to grasp how it affects our experience of the world. Vincent came home feeling cognitively and emotionally depleted. Managing his ADHD symptoms left him feeling stressed and anxious.

Operating in a modern world with its demands on planning, focusing, prioritizing, and managing time takes much more effort than many without ADHD realize, and it can feel like we're barely keeping our heads above water. Some of that exhaustion comes from working memory limitations.

If you're living with ADHD, you're likely familiar with the frustration of losing your train of thought. It's like the mental path you were following while working on a task suddenly disappears, and you resemble a hunting dog, zigzagging the terrain in search of a scent to guide you back onto the right path. This isn't solely due to distractions; it's primarily a result of the working memory impairment associated with ADHD.

Imagine your working memory as a temporary storage space in your brain. Think of it as a mental whiteboard where you jot down notes to help you keep track of your thoughts. This whiteboard also allows you to rearrange items, which is beneficial for handling complex tasks such as reasoning, problem-solving, and language comprehension. Most of us with ADHD have working memory issues that make life difficult. In other words, our whiteboards are smaller.

Working memory is mainly located in the prefrontal cortex, the part of the brain where most of us with ADHD have limited access and weaker functioning. Upon learning about his working memory

How to Support Short-Term and Working Memory Glitches

Vincent developed strategies to support his short-term and working memory issues:

1. He sets up his day and rehearses it the night before. "It's like a dress rehearsal for my brain," he says.
2. He uses digital reminders to guide him through his day. He has two different sounds on his cell phone. A gentle-sounding chime reminds him to switch activities, while the car horn alarm reminds him when to leave work or home to pick up the children.
3. He writes things down. He invested in an e-notebook to help him remember and organize. (You can use notebooks, planners, or smartphone apps to jot down important information, tasks, and reminders.)
4. He prioritizes getting adequate sleep. "I can't seem to remember anything if I'm tired." (Lack of sleep can significantly impact memory and cognitive function. Ensure you are getting enough quality sleep each night.)

Even with these strategies, Vincent will tell you that remembering is difficult. What can you do if you struggle with short-term or working memory issues?

K. C. wanted to support Vincent without nagging or treating him like a child. She implemented these strategies:

limitations, Vincent noticed that he felt like he wrote in invisible ink on his whiteboard, meaning that he thought something was there because he "wrote" it, but when he tried to read it, he said, "It just isn't there. I get so frustrated because the thought is just gone, and now I'm ornery to anyone in my radius." Cranky and frustrated with his limited working memory, Vincent latched on to negative emotions, mumbling angrily to himself at work and at home.

1. She learned to recognize the following working memory issues and not associate them with character flaws:
   - Frequently misplacing items or forgetting where they were placed.
   - Struggling to follow multistep instructions or tasks.
   - Getting easily distracted during tasks that require focused attention.
   - Having difficulty weighing options and making decisions, especially in complex situations.
   - Forgetting appointments, deadlines, or important dates.
   - Struggling with tasks that require simultaneous processing of multiple pieces of information.

2. When seeing one of the signs of Vincent's memory issues, K. C. would offer, "I think your working memory is overloaded—would you like help?"

3. She set up a "launch pad" by their back door. She designed an area where each person in their household had a place for the things they needed to leave the house. Vincent had a place for his keys, wallet, briefcase, and watch.

4. In addition to their shared digital calendar, K. C. posted the family's schedule so everyone could see it.

5. She remained committed to believing that Vincent's working memory issues weren't character flaws.

K. C. found it challenging to grasp the concept of a small whiteboard in Vincent's mind, especially when her prefrontal cortex functioned effectively. While she did have occasional lapses, like walking into a room and forgetting her purpose momentarily, her experience was notably less frequent than Vincent's. Nevertheless, she could empathize with his irritability, acknowledging, "I understand that his frustration stems from difficulties with his memory, particularly when he attempts tasks that put a strain on it." Together, they've learned strategies for communicating and assisting each other when this occurs.

Big Emotions

ADHD often involves intense emotions, yet emotions are frequently overlooked during diagnosis. In fact, the current diagnostic criteria for ADHD used by therapists does not explicitly address emotional difficulties. However, Dr. Russell Barkley, an internationally recognized authority on ADHD, ardently advocates for recognizing deficient emotional self-regulation as a fundamental aspect of ADHD, alongside challenges in behavioral and cognitive self-regulation.[1]

People with ADHD tend to experience significant emotional fluctuations, low frustration tolerance, impatience, a quick temper, and heightened excitability. Emotional intensity arises from differences in the ADHD brain, where some regions underfunction while others overfunction.

K. C. often finds herself caught in Vincent's intense emotions and mood swings, where even minor issues can escalate into major conflicts. She recounted a situation where they had planned a date night after work but had to adjust their plans due to their daughter's swimming practice, as her friend's parents couldn't drive her. "Every little detail gets magnified," she said. "Vincent was agitated and said we couldn't go out."

Vincent's anger led him to declare the evening a failure. At the same time, K. C. felt they could have adapted their plans with a bit of flexibility. Surprisingly, Vincent became angry because he was looking forward to the date night, leading to intense feelings like disappointment and frustration.

A lot of people like K. C. feel they have to be careful around their relatives with ADHD to avoid causing intense emotional reactions. Learning about the pool metaphor in chapter 12 has helped them observe their own emotional reactions and respond in better ways.

Contagious Dysregulation

Emotions in K. C. and Vincent's household are contagious, spreading like a common cold from one person to another. One way this happens is when K. C. feels overwhelmed with responsibilities at home. She believes she's shouldering the lion's share of family responsibilities due to Vincent's ADHD, effectively becoming the sole responsible adult in their home. "When I come home after working a full day, it feels like I'm running the entire show," she says. Even during weekends or vacations, she can't fully relax, always on edge, doubting whether she can trust Vincent to take care of the kids. It's as though she's forever standing guard, fearing that everything will crumble if she lets down her guard.

This constant feeling of being the "adult on duty" is a common source of frustration for spouses who don't have ADHD. K. C. highlights how Vincent doesn't contribute to household chores, pick up after himself, or even handle basic tasks like taking out the trash despite her repeated requests for help.

K. C. tries to conceal her emotions, but they seep out in passive-aggressive comments—an unhealthy way of dealing with her feelings. She admits, "I find myself ruminating about how he has let me down. I'm angry at him before he even does anything." The burden of her emotions regarding their marriage frequently becomes overwhelming for her. This is a challenging situation that many non-ADHD spouses can relate to as they grapple with balancing their love for their partner with the frustration and resentment stemming from ADHD symptoms.

Vincent is remarkably attuned to K. C.'s negative emotions, and his responses are like a mirror, reflecting whatever emotion she's experiencing. Vincent often follows suit when K. C. gets angry, leading to what they both admit are "ridiculous arguments." It's a cycle of emotional reactivity, and neither seems to have mastered self-regulation.

When faced with challenges, they respond instinctively with stress, anger, or hurt. I explore this phenomenon, which I call "survival thinking," in chapter 8. In fight-or-flight moments, our reactions intensify, and our perception of the situation becomes skewed. Survival thinking obstructs our ability to see things objectively, leading us to react impulsively rather than engage in reasoned responses or consider alternative viewpoints. K. C.'s and Vincent's behaviors are driven by emotions and defense mechanisms, resulting in a continuous loop of responding to each other's feelings. Learning to engage in transformational thinking (chapter 8) has helped them handle their challenges more productively.

Rejection Sensitivity

Vincent expressed frustration after feeling criticized by K. C., saying, "It feels like there's only one correct way to do things, and I never seem to get it right." He recounted an incident involving an innocent mix-up with sponges for cleaning, exclaiming, "How was I supposed to know that was the floor sponge?" Constant corrections have left him feeling incompetent and treated like a child. Shame crossed his face when he confided, "Sometimes I avoid taking the initiative because I anticipate her criticism. It's as if she doesn't see me as an adult." This sentiment is shared by many individuals with ADHD, who often feel micromanaged and criticized by their partners. Vincent's experience had even led to his developing rejection sensitivity, further complicating communication with K. C.

Rejection sensitivity (RS) is like a magnifying glass for emotions, intensifying the feelings of emotional sensitivity and distress in people with ADHD when they believe they're being criticized or rejected by important individuals in their lives.[2] It's crucial to understand that individuals like Vincent who experience RS aren't weak or immature; instead, they experience emotional pain much more powerfully than those without ADHD.

RS can be incredibly confining and debilitating, leading those affected to react strongly to rejection, criticism, or failure situations. It's like having your emotions dialed up to the maximum.

Common triggers for RS include the withdrawal of love, approval, or respect; playful teasing; well-intentioned criticism; and the relentless self-criticism or negative self-talk that often arises from a perceived failure.

RS can turn genuine communication of feelings and needs in a relationship into a formidable challenge. Those with RS often fear that expressing their emotions will lead to rejection, so they suppress their true feelings, which eventually culminates in explosive outbursts of anger or frustration. This cycle of suppression and eruption only leads to more misunderstandings and conflicts.

K. C. may not fully grasp Vincent's struggle with RS because when he senses rejection or threat, he frequently responds with a defensive barrage of hurtful remarks. For instance, he anticipates criticism from K. C., which he interprets as rejection, leading him to externalize his emotions and launch into angry tirades even before K. C. can speak.

Sometimes individuals with RS internalize their emotions, causing them to withdraw and retreat. One of my clients shared the feeling of constantly trying to climb out of a pit, only to have her mother inadvertently push her back by mentioning her weight gain. Consequently, she perceives judgment and rejection from her mother, leading her to avoid communication.

RS can profoundly impact all relationships, including parental and romantic ones. People with RS often experience intense anxiety, self-doubt, and negative emotions when they perceive rejection, even if it is neither accurate nor intended. In a romantic context, RS can trigger significant anxiety and insecurity about their partner's feelings and intentions, resulting in a constant fear of rejection or abandonment.

Working through RS, especially in the context of ADHD, can be challenging. Still, there are strategies and techniques that can help manage and reduce its impact on your relationships. In addition to increasing his self-awareness and communicating his experiences to K. C., Vincent learned that when he is in his window of

Feeling rejection sensitivity? Dr. Russell Ramsay suggests asking these questions:

- What situation triggered my RS? (Define in behavioral versus emotional terms.)
- What are my thoughts about this situation?
- How can I reevaluate my thoughts?
- What are my feelings about this situation?
- What are my feelings telling me, and how can I manage them?
- What am I doing or not doing to handle this situation?
- What is my implementation plan for this situation?
- How do I wield my social capital in this situation?[3]

tolerance (chapter 6) and using transformational thinking (chapter 8), he prefers dismissing his RS thinking pattern.

Remember that managing RS is an ongoing process, and it may take time to find the strategies that work best for you. Be patient with yourself and seek professional guidance if needed. It's also essential to involve your loved ones in your journey so they can provide understanding and support.

The Paradox of Sensitivity

Emotional sensitivity is often characteristic of those with ADHD due to their unique brain wiring. However, there's a paradox to this sensitivity. While those with ADHD can be exceptionally attuned to others' feelings, there are moments when they seem entirely focused on their own emotions, which can come across as inconsiderate and hurtful to those around them.[4]

Consider Sarah's experience with her twenty-something ADHD sister. When Sarah called her, her sister said, "I'm busy. Stop calling me," and promptly hung up.

Sarah couldn't help but wonder, *Why didn't she ignore the call or put her phone on Do Not Disturb? I don't understand. I know she can be kind and loving, but that hurt.* Sarah went on to explain that when her sister displayed such behavior, it left her feeling unloved. The egocentricity and insensitivity expressed by ADHD family members can lead to feelings of rejection and a misunderstanding of their actions as a lack of love.

Sarah's sister was likely overwhelmed by a task and striving to maintain focus. She saw the incoming call as a threat to her concentration. She impulsively answered the call to block out interference and snapped at Sarah. During this frantic effort to safeguard her focus (remember the small whiteboard), Sarah's feelings were not even in the equation.

Parents often describe this paradox of sensitivity by referring to their children with ADHD as "Sour Patch Kids." Like the candy's slogan, "First they're sour, then they're sweet," children with ADHD might hurl hurtful insults and accusations at family members in the heat of the moment and later tearfully apologize, seeking to make amends. It's as if when they are angry, they impulsively want to inflict pain on another person and search their minds for the most hurtful words or actions. Yet when they regain their levelheadedness, they are taken aback by their own words and actions. Overcome with remorse, they tearfully apologize.

This paradox of sensitivity adds complexity to family relationships. The repairing and reconnecting strategies recommended in chapters 19 and 20 are essential to learn if you have experienced this phenomenon.

Nurturing Healthy Relationships amid ADHD Challenges

ADHD undeniably has a significant impact on the dynamics of family relationships. We must strive for effective communication and love within our families instead of resorting to blame. Blame in any form is a destructive force that corrodes the bonds of relationships. Often people blame all their marital or familial issues on their partner's ADHD symptoms, leading to inaction and a lack of shared responsibility. I often hear grievances like, "My spouse's symptoms have torn our marriage apart and are the root of most of our arguments," and, "My partner insists it's my responsibility to fix my ADHD if we want to salvage our relationship." Sometimes parents point fingers at their child with ADHD as the source of strife within their household.

Similarly, individuals with ADHD may sometimes blame their spouses for what they perceive as a lack of empathy. While ADHD symptoms can indeed trigger relationship challenges, they are not the sole cause. How individuals respond to one another can either bolster or undermine the relationship.

Blame can potentially inflict considerable damage on a relationship by establishing a negative cycle in which one person holds the other responsible for their problems. This often prompts the accused partner to become defensive and potentially reciprocate with blame. This destructive cycle can result in lingering conflicts and festering resentment, eroding the emotional connection between partners.

When I first met Vincent and K. C., they had shifted the entire burden of change onto the other person, sidestepping personal accountability for their own emotions and actions. Blame was corroding the very foundation of their relationship, impeding progress and the healthy resolution of issues. As they grew in their understanding of ADHD and their relationship, they learned to take responsibility for their own behaviors. K. C. decided that rather than placing blame and pointing fingers at Vincent's behavior, she would acknowledge her feelings of hurt or frustration and engage in open and honest communication. She expressed her feelings by saying, "When you passed by the pile of laundry on your way to having fun, I felt frustrated and lonely, like I'm the only one who is doing housework."

Vincent, who didn't see the pile, responded, "I didn't intend that at all." They talk about getting laundry completed.

Blame leads only to defensiveness and disconnection, while sincere communication creates opportunities for collaboration and compromise.

Moving Forward Together

In many of my podcast interviews, I discuss my husband's ADHD symptoms and their impact on our relationship. Sometimes I throw in a little sarcasm, joking that, despite also having ADHD, I'm an absolute delight to live with. The awkward laugh from the host tells me that my sarcasm fell flat, landing like a soggy pancake on the floor.

My own ADHD symptoms do affect my husband. I tend to experience intense emotions that often spill out when he's trying to unwind after a long day. He's a social butterfly, while the mere thought of going out with another couple for dinner exhausts me. I might become insistent that I told him about our neighbor's cat and he should care, only to later realize that I told our daughter about it, not him. And then there's the challenge of trying to hold a thought on my small mental whiteboard. My struggles with working memory tend to manifest when I'm getting ready to leave the house. I end up doing the equivalent of answering a call with a stern "Stop calling!" expression, except directed at him as if to say, "I'm trying to think! Don't talk to me!" Like I said, I'm an absolute peach to live with.

Relationships, especially neurodiverse ones, take a great deal of work. Being part of a family affected by ADHD is undoubtedly complex. It often leaves people wondering, "Is it you, me, or ADHD?" It's easy to see how feelings on both sides can contribute to a destructive cycle within the relationship. The non-ADHD partner may resort to complaints and nagging, growing increasingly resentful, while the ADHD partner, feeling judged

43

and misunderstood, becomes defensive and withdraws. Ultimately, nobody is happy. But it doesn't have to be this way. You can cultivate healthier, more balanced behaviors that may lead to improved relationships. You can't control others, but you can enhance your self-awareness and work on your reactions.

Those with ADHD need to remember that while the distractibility, disorganization, and impulsivity commonly associated with ADHD can create challenges in various aspects of our adult lives, they can be particularly impactful when it comes to our closest relationships—our families. These symptoms often spill over into our interactions, causing family members to feel ignored, devalued, and frustrated. We may miss crucial details, agree to things without remembering, and struggle with organizational tasks, leading our loved ones to pick up the slack and fostering codependency. Our impulsivity can leave our non-ADHD family members bewildered, wondering why we act the way we do. The reminders or prompts they give may result from their frustration or stress rather than an intention to attack or criticize us.

Perhaps most significantly, our emotional outbursts can take a toll on our relationships. We must take responsibility for our symptoms and minimize their impact on those we care about.

On the flip side, those who don't have ADHD must let go of unrealistic expectations that their ADHD family members should behave as if they have fully functioning prefrontal cortexes and impeccable executive functions. While individuals with ADHD may have weaknesses in certain areas, they also possess unique strengths. Recognizing and appreciating these strengths can lead to surprising improvements in family dynamics. Allowing each person to contribute their unique "superpower" to the family can foster mutual respect and understanding. Some members may excel at planning and organization. Others may have an innate ability to sense when someone is struggling or to create memorable family activities.

It's also essential for non-ADHD family members to remember that ADHD symptoms are not character traits. Instead of labeling a family member as irresponsible, try to understand that their forgetfulness and lack of follow-through are symptoms of ADHD. When your mother is running late (just as you expected), it's likely not a deliberate attempt to annoy you but rather a manifestation of time blindness.

While it's valuable to understand the challenges of ADHD in a family, it's equally important to find ways to nurture love and build strong, enduring relationships. The goal is to create a family where every member is cherished for who they are. The first step in achieving this is acknowledging the neurological differences within your family.

In the next chapter, we'll embark on a unique journey that encourages you to envision your ADHD symptoms as mischievous monkeys and even gives you the chance to name these "monkeys." Whether you're well acquainted with your ADHD traits or just beginning to explore them, this metaphorical exercise can unveil nuanced aspects of how ADHD influences your life.

For those who don't have ADHD, this chapter will provide a valuable glimpse into the internal dialogues of individuals with ADHD, shedding light on what might seem like mysterious or perplexing behaviors. It gives an opportunity to bridge the gap in understanding and gain insight into the fascinating world of ADHD.

So get ready to meet those inner monkeys and embark on this adventure.

3

MONKEY MALARKY

The lion and big cat exhibits were fine, but those animals just lay around, occasionally flipping their tails. Impatiently, I tugged my grandfather's hand and led him to the real action. Monkey Island. It was an exhibit of monkeys and goats occupying a rocky island surrounded by a water-filled moat and a concrete wall. I pulled myself up the aggregate concrete barrier, my tennis shoes digging into the wall while I steadied myself on my elbows. A waft of the stinking animal water hit my nose. The island was full of movement. One monkey sat close to another, picked something off, examined it, and ate it! Another monkey ran in wide loops, hitting his friend on top of his head each time he passed. His friend responded by half-heartedly swatting in his direction but otherwise kept examining a parcel of food. Now, this was entertainment.

I watched how the spider monkeys used their tails to maneuver a rope between the two fake mountaintops. Although I wasn't sure how to pronounce it then, I knew from the sign nearby that they had prehensile tails. I loved how that characteristic gave the monkeys additional resourceful abilities, like a fifth limb to grab objects.

The antics of the monkeys at John Ball Zoo captured my imagination. When I visited them in my teens, I began narrating their discussions. "For cryin' out loud, Phillip, hold still while I groom you." And for the more philosophical monkey off to the side contemplating her lack of thumb as she looked longingly at her four long fingers: "What if I had an extra and opposable digit? How might that change my existence?"

Monkey shenanigans still amuse me, which is why I imagine my ADHD symptoms as monkeys leaping around in my head. Like the monkeys on the island, my ADHD symptoms are smart, cheeky little rascals who seem to take on a life of their own. Unfortunately, I don't like how their antics affect my life. Sometimes my ADHD monkeys are a nuisance; other times they can be obnoxiously problematic. Managing them takes a lot of effort.

So before diving into family dynamics and ADHD, let's look at how your ADHD affects you. Imagine having five or so monkeys at a time vying for attention. These monkeys represent your loudest ADHD symptoms or coping mechanisms. By naming the monkeys, you can directly address the issues they cause.

As you read the names and descriptions of the various ADHD monkeys, keep a list of your top five. There are three categories

Consider the top five monkeys that you work with daily:

Angry Andrew	Mopey Mike
Anxious Amy	Overwhelmed Oscar
Avoidant Ava	Perfect Penny
Bouncing Beatrice	Rejection-Sensitive Rachel
Critical Calvin	Thrill-Seeking Theodore
Disorganized Derek	Time-Blind Timmy
Helpless Hannah	
Impatient Iggy	

of monkeys: the usual suspects (the ones that we would expect to go with ADHD), the energy monkeys (the ones that have to do with energy usage), and the vexatious primates (the most bothersome ones).

The Usual Suspects

The first group of monkeys includes the ones many people are used to seeing: *Disorganized Derek*, *Impatient Iggy*, and *Time-Blind Timmy*. They run around performing their rapscallion antics. Disorganized Derek tells you not to waste time opening the mail and instead leave it in a massive heap on your foyer table. Impatient Iggy asks, "Why is this taking so long?" and "Can we hurry this up?" He's ready to move on to another activity. And then there's Time-Blind Timmy, who cannot sense the passing of time. He feels terrible whenever people mistake his sensory issue for intentionally disregarding time.

Do you see any familiar monkeys in that bunch? Remember, we are only looking at your monkeys. It's easy to name another person's monkeys, but as we'll learn later, focus on your monkeys first.

The Energy Monkeys

The second group of monkeys—*Avoidant Ava*, *Bouncing Beatrice*, *Mopey Mike*, *Overwhelmed Oscar*, and *Thrill-Seeking Theodore*—has to do with energy usage. Bouncing Beatrice and Thrill-Seeking Theodore are the monkeys many think of regarding hyperactive ADHD symptoms. Beatrice with her frenetic energy seems to dart around a room. Theodore is searching for his next dopamine rush by taking risks or starting trouble. With all their tomfoolery getting the headlines, we may forget that fatigue is one of the most common symptoms associated with ADHD.

Cue Overwhelmed Oscar. He flops on the floor in exhaustion because there's too much to do and not enough time or energy to do it all. The mere thought of having to think about thinking about an activity is often too much for this low-energy monkey. Meanwhile, Mopey Mike wanders around, not quite depressed or sad but definitely feeling burned out. He complains that he has nothing to look forward to doing.

Avoidant Ava is a quiet energy miser. Many of my clients don't even notice her presence. She comforts her host by offering activities that distract them from problematic thoughts, feelings, or actions. This monkey is a particular favorite of many teen boys holed up in their rooms or basements who are playing video games as a way of not addressing their needs or their current situations. Avoidance is a vicious self-defeating cycle, leading to more and more problems. Many of my clients immerse themselves in habits to distract or distance themselves from their present emotional experience: drinking, overeating, overexercising, binge-watching, overworking, and endless phone scrolling. Sure, this monkey keeps them busy, but while they are engaged in an avoidant task, they probably aren't learning, growing, or problem-solving because those are uncomfortable.

Avoidant Ava operates with the motto "Out of sight, out of mind." This escape-coping monkey believes she is helping you through distraction. Usually she shows up around a decision or a strong emotion. For example, do you have a choice to make that you don't want to make? Does thinking about a specific person or task make you uncomfortable? Have family members mentioned that you're avoiding a particular thing? Do you have a pattern of numbing yourself? I've spent a little more time describing this monkey because she is a challenging one to catch since she is exceptionally good at her job.

The Vexatious Primates

While all the monkeys I've mentioned can be impish in their own way and can cause trouble if unchecked, this last group of monkeys seems to cause even more severe problems: *Angry Andrew*, *Anxious Amy*, *Critical Calvin*, *Helpless Hannah*, *Perfect Penny*, and *Rejection-Sensitive Rachel*. Though they believe they are helpful monkeys, their impact can be dangerous for you and those you love.

Angry Andrew. I'm talking about the type of anger that is destructive and wreaks havoc on us and our relationships. Experts agree that anger and irritability are a fundamental part of the ADHD experience, even though those symptoms are missing from the diagnostic criteria. Many individuals with ADHD encounter excessive problems with anger, irritability, and other intense negative emotions.

Many times Angry Andrew thinks he's helping us. Sometimes anger gives us a sense of control. It protects us, our property, and our values. For example, while I was traveling last year, my new iPhone was stolen, and I was angry. Why did I become so angry? Well, what else could I do? Unlike Liam Neeson's character in the movie *Taken*, I didn't have a particular set of skills to follow the criminal and retrieve my phone. So instead of feeling helpless, I became angry, and that gave me a sense of control.

Anger also benefits those with ADHD because the intense emotion energizes us. And often that feels good. Angry Andrew helps us discharge the tension from our bodies. That's why someone with ADHD can blow up one moment and be fine the next.

Do you have this monkey in your top five? Do you generally have negative feelings toward activities, people, or things? Do you have tantrums? Can you move quickly from feeling okay to anger or frustration? Are you easily offended? Do you carry resentment? Do you threaten other people with your wrath, using it as a defense mechanism? These questions may be difficult to answer on your own; you may want to ask someone who knows you to help assess the damage this monkey may be doing. If you have this monkey, think carefully about how it affects you and others.

Anxious Amy. Anxious Amy is such a complicated monkey. Although anxiety alone is not included in the diagnostic criteria for ADHD, the link between the two conditions is substantial. (Note: I am talking about the anxiety accompanying ADHD, not generalized anxiety disorder.) Individuals with ADHD are more likely to struggle with this monkey for various reasons. The nature of ADHD often makes day-to-day life stressful, creating situations and environments ripe for worry, nervousness, restlessness, dread, and the butterflies-in-the-stomach feeling that so many of my clients describe. Our short-term and working memory issues seem to exacerbate this monkey's presence in our lives.

A client explained that he was anxious because he feared forgetting to complete a task. He was using a powerful emotion—anxiety, in this case—to try to hold on to remembering.

"Here I am in beautiful Bali," Shandra texted me, "sitting on white-sand beaches watching a Skittle-colored sunset, and all I can think about is the worry that sits on my chest. Every thought I have introduces a new issue to worry about. When I try to solve it, I get even more anxious. I can't shut this off." Shandra carried Anxious Amy on her journey to Indonesia. Our quick text conversation helped her figure out why this monkey was so present. Travel was new to her, and her senses were overwhelmed by the newness of it all. Her sensitive nervous system responded by sending Anxious Amy to guard her.

Anxiety often tries to help us by alerting us to details we may forget, directing our attention to possible threats, and reminding us of significant pieces of our daily activities. Anxious Amy is flexible. She alerts to protect us from perceived dangers, telling us to shut down in some cases but spurring us to action in others. If you have this precious but terribly misguided monkey, it often works overtime to help you.

Is Anxious Amy in your top five? Do you find it challenging to try new things or to take risks? Do you think about the trillions of ways that things can go wrong? Do you find yourself feeling caged by excessive worry? Does having anxiety help you get motivated to do something you've been putting off?

Critical Calvin. "Not now, Calvin," I mutter as I attempt to plan my day. Critical Calvin developed in third grade to help me pretend to be more of a regular kid. He reminded me, "Put your name in the top right-hand corner of the paper, or you'll lose your recess again." Of course, I obeyed because I needed help. This self-loathing monkey grew with me, and I used him as a guide to know how to proceed. Instead of learning self-compassion and forgiving myself for making mistakes, I relied on this monkey to keep me sharp and to move forward in an unfriendly world. He reports for duty regularly because he still wants to protect that scared third grader. Today, I reassure him I have skills and strategies for remembering tasks like placing my name in the upper right-hand corner of my homework.

Some of us developed Calvin as a coping mechanism to help us navigate all parts of life. He overlooks our strengths, looks at the disproportionate weight of our faults, and then uses that to motivate us. Unfortunately, the hardships Calvin can cause are as apparent as they are painful.

Critical Calvin shows up in the most underhanded of ways. Do you blame yourself for every negative situation? Do you get down on yourself as a person when you've made a mistake, instead of focusing just on the error? Have you caught yourself thinking, *I'm a failure?* Do you compare yourself with someone else—and come up short? Are you never satisfied with your achievements? Do you have impossibly high standards? Are you unable to accept compliments? Do you persistently analyze your mistakes? Have you been able to hear your constant harsh and negative self-talk? If Calvin's modus operandi sounds familiar to you, please consider finding a professional to discuss it—and add him to your top five.

Helpless Hannah. Alyson, a regional sales rep, had been told she was not working up to her potential. No matter how hard she tried, she couldn't set priorities like the company wanted her to or keep up with paperwork. Her colleagues seemed to get promoted quickly and move into leadership roles. At one point, she was afraid she would lose her job. "Nothing I do matters. I always lose," she told me when we first met. Professional life was tough for Alyson. Even after beginning treatment for ADHD, she was sure she was doomed to fail again and again. Helpless Hannah had convinced her that she was powerless and that she didn't have any control.

Many people with ADHD learn helplessness. They've spent so many years failing to live up to their potential at work, at home, and in personal relationships that they assume they will invariably flop. Many of my clients show up with Helpless Hannah on their shoulder when we talk about improving their sleep. "I've tried everything," they complain. "Nothing ever works." They grow frustrated and firmly believe that nothing they do will help, so they stop trying altogether. Arguing about the benefits of sleep will not help. Hannah has done her work well.

Helpless Hannah tries to soothe our pain when we continuously face a negative, uncontrollable situation. "Trying this hard is too difficult," she whispers. "Just accept that things are this way." Like many other monkeys, she is working to protect us.

Is Helpless Hannah hindering you? Do you find yourself expecting to fail, or not even trying because you are certain you'll somehow screw things up? Do you try to shift the blame to someone or something else when things go wrong? Have your friends compared you to Winnie-the-Pooh's companion Eeyore, the gloomy gray donkey?

Perfect Penny. This precision-minded primate meticulously crafts lofty standards for herself—and the other monkeys. Many of us have Perfect Penny to help us juggle the challenges of ADHD, including lack of attention and focus, impulsivity, and hyperactivity. Driven by societal expectations and personal benchmarks, Penny pressures her primate pals, exhorting them to cast themselves in the most flattering light.

Imagine how the other monkeys irritate her. The sight of Avoidant Ava, with her penchant for procrastination, sends shivers down

Penny's impeccably groomed fur. A perpetual cycle ensues: Penny creates lists of unrealistic goals, Ava leisurely procrastinates, and into the fray steps Overwhelmed Oscar, who wants to stop all activity. Then Penny escalates her demands.

Whenever I find myself getting irritated with my ADHD symptoms, I stop and listen for Perfect Penny. And there she is, complaining, "If these dumb monkeys would just stop being themselves . . ."

How do you know when Perfect Penny is trying to help you manage your monkeys? Are you overly critical of yourself, even when others consider your work or efforts satisfactory? Do you find it challenging to complete tasks because you're constantly refining and adjusting them to meet extremely high standards? Do you set goals for yourself that are often difficult or nearly impossible to achieve? Do you find accepting compliments or positive feedback difficult, constantly feeling like there's room for improvement? Do you struggle with procrastination due to the fear that you won't be able to complete a task perfectly?

Rejection-Sensitive Rachel. We were introduced to this monkey in chapter 2 with Vincent's story. Many of my clients describe this monkey as one of the most harmful. Rejection-sensitive dysphoria is extreme emotional sensitivity when you think you're being rejected. Though not part of a formal ADHD diagnosis, it is a brain-based symptom that is likely an inherent feature of ADHD. Rejection-Sensitive Rachel is on the lookout for you when you are in danger. When she locks her sights on a real or perceived threat, she'll shift your mood to angry, sad, anxious, or whatever else to release the pain of the rejection. After the emotional release, she's satisfied that she's done her work and will disappear—until the next time.

"It's like having a wound that won't heal," Myles shared. "I am extremely sensitive to negative feedback. I know that I overreact to the slightest criticism." He developed an intense preoccupation with what others thought of him and assumed the worst in everyday interactions. "One time I listened to a voicemail from my supervisor saying, 'Please call me.' I was sure that I was going to be fired. Instead, she called to ask my opinion on a project." Myles groaned. "I feel awful so much of the time." He explained how having this monkey has limited him in so many ways. He has lost friends and romantic relationships because of it. "I don't take even the smallest risk because of my fear of failure."

Rachel knows our sensitivity, so she tries to help. She suggests perfectionistic or people-pleasing habits for us to adopt to prevent the pain of rejection. She coaches us to shrug, smile, and add pre-emptive phrases like, "I hope that makes sense," "Sorry to bother you," and "It's just a thought." Her favorite line to feed me is, "I'm okay with whatever," even when I'm not okay with whatever.

Is Rejection-Sensitive Rachel whispering in your ear? Do you have sudden emotional flare-ups following real or perceived criticism or rejection? Do you withdraw from social situations? Do you avoid social settings in which you might fail or be criticized? Do you struggle with low self-esteem and poor self-perception? Have you experienced relationship issues, especially frequently feeling attacked and responding defensively? Do you ruminate or perseverate on what another person thinks about you? Do you find yourself using Rachel's favorite tools—perfectionism and people pleasing?

Now look at your list again and select the top five. "But I have all of them!" is what you'll probably say as you listen to or read this chapter. Yes, you might. You need to focus on the most frequent ones in your life. There will be time to search for more monkeys, but for now, don't choose more than five for this exercise. When you have the list of your most frequent visitors, find an example for each monkey of when it is most active and how it is trying to help you.

Monkey Talk

Now that you have rounded up your five (or fewer) monkeys, let's look at how they relate to one another. Your monkeys are social and love lending a hand to each other almost as much as they love assisting you. Learning how your monkeys interact will help you address your ADHD symptoms more effectively.

A month before my first book launched, Rejection-Sensitive Rachel showed up in a panic. "What have you done?" she exclaimed. "Do you realize that you let people see you through this book? All that Brené Brown vulnerability stuff is utter nonsense! You said too much! What if people hate your book? What if they hate *you*?" In sheer panic, she summoned Anxious Amy, who doesn't usually make a daily appearance.

"She's right," Amy said in her sympathetic but urgent tone. "I'm deeply concerned for you."

Hearing all the commotion, Critical Calvin showed up. He couldn't miss a good drama. "You've really done it this time." He shook his head. "You are not a writer. What made you think you could do this? Now it's out there for everyone to see. You are an impostor; you don't know what you're talking about."

The three started chattering all at once until I was shaking and on the verge of tears.

Oh gosh, the monkeys are right. Can I call the publisher and back out of all this? I wondered, even though I knew that wasn't an option because the book had already been printed. Then I took a deep breath. I had agreed with my ADHD monkeys. I forgot that I am not a monkey; I have better thinking skills than those lovable knuckleheads. So I started to address them individually.

First, Anxious Amy: "Thank you for being concerned. Writing a book is a scary new thing that I'm doing. I'm going to be okay." I knew she would return later and I'd need to be ready to send her away again. Next, Rejection-Sensitive Rachel: "I agree with you. I've taken a big risk and it could lead to embarrassment, but for my own growth, I've decided to write the book." And for the moment, she too left. Finally, there was Calvin, my oldest frenemy: "Calvin, I understand that you are trying to protect me. Your negativity is too much for me. Stop." He glared and then walked away.

I had internal dialogues like this at least six more times that day and on subsequent days. It was hard work keeping those monkeys at bay until the book launched.

What conversations do your monkeys have? Do any of them have alliances? Or do any protect the other monkeys? Take a moment to think through the interactions that your monkeys have. Writing out the dialogue often helps my clients see how their symptoms compound.

Sometimes our monkeys fight or act in opposition to one another. Kiran reflected on her monkeys' conversation from the past morning. "As soon as my alarm goes off, Overwhelmed Oscar greets me, already nervous, reminding me of all that I have to do and that I can't get it all done. Then Critical Calvin appears, saying, 'You know he's right. You can't do this. In fact, I should probably remind you of all the times you've failed. Or should I begin with all the people you have let down?' He unfurls a list that rolls past his feet." Kiran imitates the face that she imagines Calvin making, her brow furrowed.

"Fortunately, Avoidant Ava appears, sending the others away. 'She doesn't need that. She needs some morning me time. Here's your phone. How about we open TikTok?'

"Time-Blind Timmy glances at an imaginary watch and nods. 'That checks out.'

"Then, half an hour later, storming back in is Calvin. 'You idiot! Get out of bed now! You've already screwed up this day! Move! Move!'

"Avoidant Ava argues, 'Just one more video!'"

Kiran shakes her head. "It's a nasty way to wake up."

The most important thing to do is identify the rascals and appreciate how they affect you. Sometimes asking your monkeys, "Why are you here?" and "How do you think you are helping me?" will help you develop a deeper understanding of their behavior and lead you to steps in minimizing their actions. Remember, only you can manage your monkeys.

Learning about Your Monkeys

If you have ADHD, take a moment to find your four or five most frequent monkeys. Feel free to add your own ADHD-related monkey. If you don't have ADHD, look at the list of monkeys and see if you have any that pop out frequently. (Keep your eyes on your own zoo right now; don't name your family members' monkeys.)

- For each monkey you identified, find an example of when it is the loudest.
- Think about how each monkey is trying to help you in its naive monkey way.
- Do any of your monkeys have alliances?
- Do any protect the other monkeys?
- Do any fight with each other?
- What insights do you have about your ADHD after identifying your monkeys?
- How are you addressing the monkey business in your head?

In the next chapter, we'll explore primary and secondary emotions and how our big ADHD emotions create difficulties for us. Then in chapter 5, we'll learn about some of the emotional errors that our monkeys may want to hang on.

A WORD OF CAUTION: After reading this chapter, you may have uncovered new insights about your ADHD. While your excitement may tempt you to share those insights and label others with their challenges, please refrain. Read the rest of part 1 and you will understand the importance of focusing on your own growth first. This advice also applies to parents dealing with children of any age.

4

UNDERSTANDING
THE STORY OF EMOTIONS

Which Greek myth do your ADHD emotions most remind you of? Do you feel like Atlas, bearing the weight of the world on your shoulders? Or do you feel like Sisyphus, doomed for eternity to roll an immense boulder up a hill, only for it to roll back down every time it nears the top? Or are you more like Prometheus, chained to a rock, and every day an eagle (or other winged bird representing life's tedious tasks) comes and eats a part of your liver? And although your liver regrows each night, your energy is fully taken from you each day.

ADHD often brings a whirlwind of intense emotions that can make us feel like we're enduring some legendary punishment. The struggle to process these emotions can seem like an immense burden, a colossal force to reckon with, or even a drain on our very life essence. Our response varies—sometimes we hold on to these feelings tightly, other times we get carried away by them, and occasionally we harness them as motivation. But here's the twist: It is not the sheer existence of these mythical-sized feelings that creates problems. It's how we interpret and react to them that cranks up their intensity even more and makes them seem unmanageable. This chapter will challenge you to think differently about your emotions as you navigate your emotional odyssey.

Before we go into the specifics about emotions, we need to remember that neurodiverse family members have a unique way of handling emotions in their brains. When the neurotypical brain encounters worry, it activates the limbic system—the part of the brain in charge of emotions and behavior. The limbic system then passes the message to the cerebral cortex, the brain region responsible for reasoning, problem-solving, and regulating emotions. Finally, the cerebral cortex, particularly the prefrontal cortex, steps in. It acts as a mediator, slowing down the emotional response long enough for a deep breath and thoughtful consideration.

But here's where the ADHD brain differs. The connection between the limbic center and the cerebral cortex is not as strong in our brains, so our ability to manage and regulate emotions takes a hit. When we experience anger, anxiety, or sadness, there's no mediating pause for a deep breath and reflection. Instead, it's as if we're gripping the safety bars of a roller coaster as our emotions take us on a wild ride—sharp turns, steep slopes, and even inversions. These emotions rush through our minds and bodies, and calming down afterward becomes a real challenge. Managing and responding to the intensity of our emotional experiences take extra effort, but we can learn to do it. Our goal isn't to stop experiencing emotions but instead to understand their significance in our lives and to decipher the story they are telling us.

The Incredible Power of Emotions

Instead of seeing our emotions as burdens, let's imagine them as a superpower that helps us understand the world around us quickly and efficiently. In his book *Emotional: How Feelings Shape Our Thinking*, physicist Leonard Mlodinow reveals that emotions are like a precious gift that enables us to "quickly and efficiently make sense of our circumstances so that we can react as necessary."[1] Emotions serve as a means to understand ourselves, connect with others, and navigate our world, providing significance and purpose to our experiences by helping us grasp our values.

Although some emotions are just fleeting feelings, sometimes they are waving a flag to get your attention. Kira was very annoyed because her cousin often canceled plans, saying to me, "Whenever we plan to go out, I expect her to cancel." By digging deeper, Kira discovered that her value of dependability was being bumped. She liked being a dependable person, and she wanted others to be dependable too. Her irritation was a signal telling her that something that mattered to her was disturbed. Understanding this helped her see why she was so frustrated with her cousin or anyone else whom she thought was being irresponsible.

Emotions also serve as clues that provide insights into our internal state. "I'm not sure why I feel sad when I see all the trees cut down on a lot," a client said. "It happens to me a lot." I encouraged her to be curious and to investigate that feeling. Two weeks later, she explained, "I talked with my therapist about the sadness. I didn't realize how much it could tell me. First, I love the environment. I hate to see natural habitats destroyed. It makes me sad. But there's also a memory of my parents building a house on a wooded lot. They had to clear many of the trees. We never lived there because they separated before the house was finished. My life became more complicated after that." She learned more about her inner landscape when she examined what she was feeling. Emotions can be an important source of personal growth and development.

Some emotions are like lightning-fast messengers, helping you react without even thinking. For example, despite your mother's instruction to use a glass, you drink milk straight out of the container. Yuck! Disgust instantly jumps in, warning you about the spoiled milk. Emotions like these prompt you to act, whether it's seeking joy or avoiding potential problems like ingesting any more of the lumpy science project sitting in your refrigerator.

Last but not least, emotions are your trusty partner when you learn. They influence your perception, attention, learning, memory, reasoning, and problem-solving. As a young high school teacher, I noticed students learned better when emotions were part of the lesson. This belief was reinforced when a former student stopped me at the mall. "Hey, you were my teacher!" the twenty-something exclaimed. I could see that he was searching for my name, which wasn't a surprise because I had him in my class only briefly before he transferred to another school. Before I could say it, he processed his thoughts verbally. "You made your sister eat dog food when you were kids; now she's a zookeeper." He laughed.

I tried to interrupt his recollection and clarify that I didn't make my sister eat dog food. I merely placed a bowl of All-Bran cereal on the floor and asked her to be a dog for a day. And the fact that she was a zookeeper is unrelated to my asking her to be my dog. But he remembered those details because the story was funny to him.

"We had a sword fight when we read a play," he continued, searching his episodic memory. "That king who got his head cut off. His wife was crazy. She was manipulative." He was using the emotions to recall memories. The sword fight that we'd acted out at the end of the play was fun and interesting, and now it worked to anchor his memory. I watched him jump from emotion to emotion as he recalled a Shakespearean play that had little relevance to his daily life.

Emotions help us remember and understand things deeply—even though that student still couldn't recall my name. Although everyone uses emotional memory, our neurodiverse family members rely on it to recall information.

Emotions reveal to us our thoughts, attitudes, behaviors, and overall well-being. They can help us learn, grow, and build meaningful relationships. We need to learn to understand what they may be telling us. In order to do that, we need to understand the two types of emotions.

Unveiling the Story

Our feelings unfold in two layers: primary and secondary. Learning about their differences will help you discover a deeper emotional story. Primary emotions are the rapid first responders. They act instinctively and swiftly, without stopping to think. Primary emotions include joy, distress, anger, fear, surprise, and disgust. Remember when you took a sip of spoiled milk straight from the carton? That immediate disgust was your primary emotion, urging you to stop immediately.

Renowned emotional psychologist Paul Ekman made a remarkable discovery. Primary emotions are like a universal expressive language understood by people across different cultures. Even members of a remote tribe in New Guinea, who had never encountered Westerners, could identify primary emotions just by looking at photos of the Americans' faces. They could mimic the corresponding facial expressions. This suggests that primary emotions are like a code shared by humans worldwide.

Unlike primary emotions, secondary emotions don't rush into action; they take time to process and require some thinking. Though there are many, secondary emotions include love, guilt, shame, embarrassment, pride, envy, and jealousy. These emotions follow the lead of our primary emotions and add depth and explanation to our emotional storyline. They usually come with a backstory, like the layers of a complex narrative. For example, while fear is a primary emotion, hate is secondary. A client shared her story of a terrifying encounter with a spider, which triggered her primary emotions of fear and surprise. "One time while I was moving firewood, a huge wolf spider climbed off the piece of wood and ran up my arm," she shared. Then she said, "I hate spiders," backing her fear with her personal narrative.

Secondary emotions are like protective shields, concealing our more vulnerable primary emotions. They create a barrier between us and the outside world, often sending mixed signals about what we truly need. Imagine this scenario: You're sad and longing for support and closeness. Instead of expressing the primary emotion, sadness, you switch to a secondary emotion like frustration and exclaim to a family member, "You never help me!" This emotional switch can confuse others, pushing them away when you need their comforting presence. It's like using a shield when a warm hug would suffice.

Once you become familiar with primary and secondary emotions, you'll be able to ask questions that will unveil the emotional story. When your child declares, "I hate school!" you'll realize they're sharing their feelings. Instead of dismissing their words and reminding them that they like lunch and recess, you can help them identify the primary emotion, like distress, by saying, "It seems like you're really frustrated. How can I help you?" This opens the door to addressing the problem.

Navigating and processing emotions often feels like a significant challenge, burdening us with the weight of an existential struggle or draining our vital life essence. Learning to understand and respond to our emotions helps us handle them better. The distinction between primary and secondary emotions allows us to process our emotional experiences without shouldering the colossal burden like Atlas carrying the world. Instead of facing an uphill battle

Primary emotions are the first instinctive emotions that you feel for any given event. Secondary emotions are feelings you experience after primary emotions. Secondary emotions usually are longer lasting and are protective of you.

Primary Emotions	Secondary Emotions
Examples: joy, distress, anger, fear, surprise, and disgust	Examples: love, guilt, shame, embarrassment, pride, envy, and jealousy
They are reactive, sensitive, and vulnerable.	They are learned, protective, and defensive.

Emotional management is knowing what we are feeling, exploring why we are feeling it, and choosing what we want to do about it.

like Sisyphus, constantly pushing a boulder that rolls back down, we can stop fighting it and consider the big emotion in front of us. We can embrace our curiosity to decipher the messages embedded in the massive emotional rock. When we do, it will transform the experience from a seemingly endless and exhausting cycle to a meaningful exploration.

Finally, when we feel like Prometheus, shackled to a stone and our liver getting pecked at every day, secondary emotions may be gnawing at our core. If you can, figure out where your secondary emotions are coming from. Ask yourself, "What's the story they're telling? Is there a different story that makes sense too? Can I change the emotional story that I am telling myself?" When you take the time to interview your emotions, you will often recover your flexibility and strength. And then, like a phoenix rising from the ashes, your emotional resilience can return, even after tough times.[2]

Dig Deep

Use these questions to determine whether the emotion you're experiencing is primary or secondary.

1. Is what I'm feeling a direct reaction to an external event? [Primary]
2. Is the emotion I'm feeling becoming more intense over time? [Secondary]
3. Am I experiencing the emotional reaction more frequently than the event that prompted it? [Secondary]

4. When the event subsided, did my emotional reaction also reduce? [Primary]

5. Is the emotional reaction I'm having continuing long after the event that caused it? Is it interfering with my abilities in the present moment? Has it been affecting new experiences? [Secondary]

6. Is what I'm feeling complex, ambiguous, or difficult to understand? [Secondary]

A first step in understanding your emotions is learning how to deal with a little bit of discomfort in order to feel better. At the first sense of "I don't like this," take a breath. Being curious about your emotions opens up the possibility of releasing or changing your feelings.

1. Start by asking, "What am I feeling?"

2. Then ask, "What is the secondary emotion that I am feeling? What story is supporting it?" Remember, secondary emotions are the explanations for the primary ones.

3. Allow yourself to wonder how the feeling surfaced. "Is there something more sensitive underneath? What is the primary emotion connected to it?"

5

EVERYDAY EMOTIONAL MISSTEPS

Emotions, those intricate and powerful facets of our inner lives, are often the driving force behind our thoughts, actions, and decisions. They shape how we perceive the world and influence how we interact. In the last chapter, we talked about how emotions can be our guides, helping us navigate our experiences and relationships. But there are moments when our emotions can mislead us.

Emotional errors come in many forms and are often subtle and insidious. These errors include misunderstandings about our feelings, miscommunication when we talk to others about our emotions, and even hiding our true feelings. They can slow down our personal growth, cause trouble in our relationships, and affect our overall well-being. But here's the good news: we can learn to avoid these errors, giving ourselves the power to make wiser choices and build deeper connections with ourselves and the people around us. Ultimately, dealing with emotional errors isn't just about personal growth; it's a crucial part of our journey to create a happier and more harmonious family life.

Emotional Error 1: Fearing Your Emotions

If sports cars represented positivity, Blaine was a Lamborghini. "Positivity has a big impact on your physical and mental health," he said, defending his approach to life. "Why focus on the negatives when there's so much good?" He made an art of reducing or ignoring many of his primary emotions and swapped negative secondary emotions for positive ones. He found the good in any given situation. After an electrical fire damaged more than half of his house, he said, "The firefighter told me that if I hadn't called them when I did, the whole place would have gone up in flames. I am so fortunate!"

"You are!" I celebrated with him, genuinely grateful for his family's safety and that his house wasn't a total loss. "How is the rest of your family doing?"

"My wife is pretty upset. She lost all her family's photos, documents, and keepsakes in the attic where the fire started." He sighed. "So . . . she's sad." Then, as if swiping away his gloomy thoughts, he said, "But I don't want to dwell on that." His relentless optimism reframed negatives into positives without much conscious effort. Blaine wanted to feel happy and satisfied most of the time. His ADHD fed this desire by boosting his dopamine whenever he concentrated on fun and positive emotions.

Blaine understood that his wife was sad, but he avoided the possibility of negativity at all costs, keeping his distance from her and her feelings. Instead, he kept himself busy with plans to rebuild and repair parts of their house, creating excitement and other upbeat sentiments over the new possibilities.

Because many of us with ADHD deeply feel things, we may decide to manage ourselves by avoiding undesirable emotions like Blaine does. He avoided the deeper parts of himself (and life) to stay comfortable. His focus on pleasure to avoid pain eventually created more pain (or problems) for himself and his relationships.

While Blaine avoided negative emotions, Mabel avoided emotions altogether. Mabel was a college sophomore at the University of Michigan. "I need to figure out how to manage my ADHD when I'm at school," the studious young woman answered when I asked about her reason for wanting ADHD coaching. She listed her executive function liabilities: trouble organizing course materials, establishing laundry and grocery shopping routines, setting study schedules, and balancing sorority activities with her studies.

When I asked about the ADHD symptoms affecting her, she didn't mention anything about emotional regulation, so I said, "Many people with ADHD feel emotions more intensely. How do you think—"

She shook her head before I finished the sentence. "No, I'm fine. I just need help organizing."

As the weeks went on, I learned that Mabel was adept at avoiding discussions where she thought she might experience distress or other strong positive or negative emotions. She shied away from her intense emotions to avoid getting overwhelmed and shutting down. She learned to be highly restrained and guarded about her feelings and instead focused her attention on her goals. Her parents praised her for her levelheaded approach to life. "It's hard to believe that she even has ADHD; she just plows through school," they marveled.

Mabel believed that her emotions were distractions that she couldn't afford. When her grandmother unexpectedly passed away midsemester, she focused even more on school to escape her sadness. Mabel became cynical and pessimistic about life, slipping sarcastic comments into our conversations. I could tell she was hurting, but she kept it buried. Her friendships suffered because she'd burst into an angry fit if she was frustrated. Although Mabel didn't self-medicate with drugs, alcohol, or gambling like many of my other clients do when they are imprisoned by this emotional error, she numbed her feelings by mindlessly scrolling TikTok and Instagram.

Suppressing or ignoring our primary emotions produces secondary emotions such as stress, anxiety, and depression. We drive them into the corners of our bodies for storage. And there they remain trapped, smoldering and stinking like a trash fire.

Ironically, both Mabel and Blaine appeared emotionally regulated, but their emotional avoidance prevented them from accessing valuable information about themselves, their desires, and their relationships. To avoid this error, they needed to build a tolerance for feeling all their emotions.

At the first sense of "I don't like this feeling," take a breath and take an interest in the emotion. Sometimes my clients visualize themselves talking to a personification of it, like they would to an ADHD monkey from chapter 3. Remaining curious about your feelings will allow you to grow.

1. Start by asking, "What am I feeling?"
2. Allow yourself to wonder, "Where is this emotion coming from?"
3. Then ask, "How did I come to feel this way?"
4. And finally, ask about the primary emotion: "Is there something more sensitive underneath?"

Asking these questions can be difficult to do in the moment of an intense emotion, so it's a good idea to examine your feelings in writing.

Emotional Error 2: Following Your Heart

As I drove home late one night after working a very long day, a conversation began in my head. "We are tired and have been a grown-up all day. We deserve some french fries for being such an adult," my emotions said. Eating french fries, for me, feels like an indulgent act of rebellion. "We really deserve this," my emotions urged.

"Eating this late will keep you up. And fast food is terrible for you," my reason answered, knowing that my emotions would write a check that my digestive system couldn't cash.

I imagined the crinkled, fried, salty, golden goodness and headed for the drive-through. What felt good suddenly felt right. "We're tired and want to be comforted," my emotions decided. I gave in to the emotional error of trusting my feelings and believed, for a short time, that it was the same thing as the right thing to do.

In movies and other media, the idea of following your heart to pursue your dreams is promoted. The hero of these stories, typically an underdog, goes against societal norms, overcomes obstacles, and wins the love of their life because they followed their heart. Friends may also advise you to "trust your heart," implying that your intense feelings are valid and true.

In reality, however, following our feelings is not always wise. While emotions can provide us with valuable information, they should not control our actions. We need to dissect our primary emotions from our secondary ones because we know that our secondary emotions can distract us from a better form of action.

Individuals with ADHD often fall into the trap of relying on emotional reasoning, accepting emotions as facts. The combination of emotional intensity and impulsivity can lead to poor decision-making. It is important to remember that emotions are often short-lived and can dissipate quickly.

Janice talked about her online shopping habit. "Sometimes I am convinced that if I get this new gadget, it will improve my life. I jump down a rabbit hole, read articles and reviews, and become even more committed to buying the item." She stopped and looked at me. "I really think I'm being rational when shopping." Janice was learning to detect emotional reasoning because her credit card debt was increasing. She shifted in her seat and explained her learning. "Here's what I've found: if I leave something in my cart for twenty-four hours, most of the time I won't buy it." Janice was getting rocketed away by a dopamine surge, and her emotional reasoning fueled it.

It is a mistake to believe that whatever you feel must be true. You might be walking down the street and think, *I feel anxious, so I know something dangerous is going to happen*, or, *I feel so depressed; this must be the worst place to work*. It's like you're saying to yourself, "I feel, therefore it is," rather than looking at what real evidence there may be. There might be no other evidence to suggest that something dangerous might happen, or that your workplace is the worst place to work. The only evidence you may be using is how you feel.

I had a client who became jealous and thought her boyfriend had feelings for someone else. "You have this feeling, but that doesn't make it true," I reminded her.

"But it feels true," she replied. She, like other perceptive ADHD folks, felt as if she was picking up vibes. I encouraged her to test her emotions before considering them as fact. When I asked her about her feeling a week later, she wasn't sure what I was talking about, then said, "Oh, that. I think I was feeling insecure that day." Feelings change.

Turning the Error on Ourselves

Sometimes we apply this error to ourselves and allow our negative feelings about ourselves to become our narrative, creating beliefs that are inconsistent with reality. When our feelings become false beliefs, we forget that we may not have evidence behind them.

Each session with Brandon seemed to end with the same recurring certainty. "Nobody likes me. I am so lonely," the high school senior told me.

My heart ached for him because he felt so intensely lonely and sad. As we talked, he conceded that he did have friends who would ask him to hang out. But his feelings about his social life created his actual view of the situation, regardless of any information to the contrary. After several sessions of this, it became apparent that he was unable to budge from the story he had created. I referred him to a therapist I knew to help him with cognitive behavioral therapy.

Have you ever punished yourself with faulty emotional reasoning? Emotional reasoning often employs many negative cognitive filters to sustain it, such as catastrophizing and disqualifying positive facts. There are so many examples of how we turn emotional reasoning inward and punish ourselves. Here are a few to help you recognize your pattern:

- "I am an awful student," you say, even when you are earning good grades. Your feelings of being overwhelmed define the reality of your academic achievements.
- "I am disgustingly overweight," you say, even though you work to maintain a healthy body by eating nutritiously, exercising, and losing weight. Shame, self-worth, or disgust with yourself becomes entangled in the truth.
- "I am only as successful as my next sale/project/performance," you say. Your feelings of worthlessness become your reality instead of the fact of past successes.

How This Error Hurts Our Relationships

Emotional reasoning can damage our relationships when our feelings about a person create our reality. Cecilia assured me that her sister was perfect in every possible way. Leah was the good-looking, goal-driven, good-student-with-tons-of-friends child, while Cecilia felt as if she was the struggled-and-still-failed child. She fixated on her sister's successes and compared them to her own. Unfortunately, her jealousy became the storyline for every interaction in her family. She blamed her mother for preferring Leah, yelled at her father for defending Leah, and found fault with her sister every chance she had. Her feelings led her to believe that she was unloved. Her actions based on her feelings drove more of a wedge between her and her family.

Many of us with ADHD prefer emotional reasoning because it seems natural. But the truth is, we can't always believe everything we feel. Sometimes strong emotions are covering up what we're really feeling. Listen for the messages your emotions are providing and examine them to help inform you. Balancing your thoughts and decision-making with your head, heart, and gut will provide the best outcomes.

The Value of Intuition

At this point most of my ADHD readers are wondering about the difference between intuition and emotions. Intuition is when you have the ability to immediately understand something without conscious reasoning. In other words, answers and solutions come to you, but you may not be aware why or how. Your brain is constantly working behind the scenes, recognizing patterns in everything you experience, without you even realizing it. There are many theories about what parts of the brain are working together to accomplish this mysterious process of having a gut feeling. Those of us with ADHD are perceptive, often without knowing it, collecting data without understanding how we acquired it.

Margot has spent years working through the difference between her emotions and intuition. She explained the difference between her feeling of anxiety and intuition. "Anxiety feels noisy and overwhelming in my head. I have a flood of thoughts and fears swishing around, and it's difficult to think clearly. Intuition makes me feel grounded and focused. The noise goes away, and I just know what to do."

Learn to identify your intuition. You can begin the same way you would test an emotion. Ask yourself, "What is the secondary emotion I'm feeling? Is this influencing my sense of intuition?"

Emotional Error 3: Blaming Things or People for How You Feel

Today Josh was going to be late for school—again. His twelfth tardy meant he would have to serve an in-house detention. While in the kitchen, the high school senior sputtered nasty insults to anyone in his vicinity and then slammed a cupboard door, yelling to no one in particular, "I hate this family!"

Josh was late again simply because he didn't wake up on time. One would think he could blame only himself for his lack of timeliness. Yet the whole house was held hostage by Josh's big emotions. It was his father's fault for not ensuring he was awake. It was his car's fault for needing time to warm up on a cold winter day. And his siblings were just idiots who made his life difficult. The list went on. Josh was blaming anyone and anything he could. He didn't want to admit fault, especially when there were easy targets to whom he could direct his ire.

We don't have to change if we can blame someone or something. We feel released from solving the problem.

All of us blame things and people for our feelings more than we think we do. Research suggests that we are naturally wired to blame others or circumstances when things go wrong.[1] Positive events are processed by the prefrontal cortex. It tends to conclude that good things happen by coincidence. Conversely, adverse events are processed by the amygdala (in the limbic system). It rapidly surmises that bad things happen on purpose and demands an explanation. This error sneaks in because it happens so quickly that we don't even notice we're acting on incomplete information. We just know that the person or thing closest to the problem must have done it on purpose!

So are those of us with ADHD better blamers because of our overreliance on the limbic system? I'm not concluding that, but we need to be aware of this tendency we have.

This error slinks in when we least expect it. Imagine you ask a seemingly innocuous question like, "Are you planning on taking the trash out tonight?" Your family member is insulted that you asked them. They begin ranting about how you nag them: "Do you think I'm stupid?" They make it clear that you upset them.

You now have your own emotions to contend with—confusion, resentment, anger, and sadness. "I only asked if you were planning to do it!" you finally snap. "I am sick of you blowing up each time I ask a simple question." You are filled with righteous indignation.

Where's the blame? Obviously, your family member is blaming you for how they are feeling. But in this story, you also blame your family member for your feelings. Unfortunately, this is a perpetual cycle in many families. It is crucial to understand that our interpretation of things, not the things or people themselves, generates emotions. By recognizing and addressing emotional errors, we can remain calm and manage our emotions more effectively, even in situations where others are struggling.

Like many of our emotional habits, the tendency to blame others can be traced to our families of origin. We may have learned this strategy by observing parents who modeled it. For example, a parent may tell a child, "You are making me so angry right now." That parent is modeling a lack of responsibility for their own emotions. Or a parent may slam a door, saying, "Stupid door always sticks!" As a result, the child learns to find scapegoats (things or people) for their emotions.

To confront this emotional mistake, be vigilant and take responsibility for your own emotions. When you experience a secondary feeling, observe your quick thinking toward blaming something or someone. Learn that mistakes happen, acknowledge them, and move into problem-solving. This ensures you are less likely to be caught blaming.

A family I worked with realized they had a culture of not taking responsibility for their emotions. When the family camped and mountain biked together, they noticed that they developed

For Parents

Asking "Who's at fault?" encourages blaming. Instead, try to find out where the process broke down. Very often, issues can be addressed by examining what went wrong. The pool metaphor in chapters 12 and 13 will provide more tools for managing this error.

a pattern of snipping at each other over things that weren't packed correctly, broken equipment, and other inconveniences. "Setting up camp is so tense," one of their teenagers told me. So they conducted a "lessons learned" debrief at the campfire to understand what went wrong. They avoided assigning blame and instead tried to find solutions. Since their whole family had ADHD and would likely forget the lessons learned due to their short-term and working memory issues, they kept notes on their phones.

The family culture began to change. When their twelve-year-old took a nasty fall off his bike on one of those trips, in the past he would have blamed his "cheap" bike and demanded a more expensive one. This time he explained, "I didn't account for the sand and the roots and the bottom of the hill. Lesson learned." He understood what went wrong and would ride his bike with a different strategy. The family changed how they interacted with things and people by addressing this emotional error head-on.

Emotional Error 4: Judging Your Feelings

Elizabeth confessed to being frustrated with her stepson. She looked at me and said, "I know I shouldn't feel that way."

I winced and interrupted, "What do you mean you 'shouldn't feel that way'?"

She shrugged. "I don't know. It's just wrong to think like that." She stared out the window.

So many of my clients make the emotional error of judging an emotion. Elizabeth had practiced taking her secondary emotions not at face value or as truth but simply as emotions and information. She was working on breaking the emotional habit of becoming easily irritated with family members. Instead of being curious about the emotion and considering where it came from, she shamed herself for even having it. When she judged herself negatively for feeling frustrated, she added guilt to her irritation, compounding her emotional weight. When secondary emotions stack up, they leave us confused and overwhelmed.

There is a difference between taking responsibility for your emotions and judging them. Taking responsibility means you seek to understand the secondary and then the primary emotion, knowing you have some control over how you express your feelings. Remember, all emotions serve as a billboard announcing a message. Listen for what that message may be and decide how to respond. Taking responsibility for your feelings means holding yourself accountable for your big emotions spilling in front of or onto another person. When you respond to emotions with judgment, you leave less room for curiosity and understanding.

> When secondary emotions stack up, they leave us confused and overwhelmed.

When you notice yourself passing judgment on your feelings, consider these strategies to help you engage with them more effectively:

1. *Check if they're real.* Take a moment to determine whether your emotions are a response to a genuine threat or just how you perceive things.
2. *Think about consequences.* Consider what might happen if you ignore your emotions. Recognizing and accepting your feelings, even the tough ones, can be a way to comfort yourself and not rely on others for validation.
3. *Look for insights.* Understand that your emotions can reveal necessary information about what's going on deep down.
4. *Remember they're temporary.* Remind yourself that emotions don't last forever. It's easy to feel stuck, but that can change quickly. The goal is to experience all your feelings without letting them define who you are.

Emotional Error 5: Believing That If You Don't Have a Strong Emotion, You Must Be Sad or Depressed

All of us can fall victim to this error. When we feel ambiguous or uncertain, our brains unconsciously choose pessimistic emotions.[2] Those of us with ADHD are accustomed to having many big emotions ricocheting in our heads. When we lack energy or are tired, ill, unmedicated, or bored, our emotions may be calmer, so we feel like something is lacking. Most of my clients have told me at one time or another, "I think there's something wrong with me—I don't have any big emotions. Could I be depressed?" I asked them to consider three categories that could help them identify their feelings and situation: depression, sadness, and lack of big emotions.

Depression is a mental health disorder characterized by persistent feelings of sadness, hopelessness, and loss of interest in activities that were once enjoyable. It lasts longer than two weeks and can significantly impact a person's life. It can affect their thoughts, feelings, behavior, and overall physical health. Symptoms of depression can vary from person to person but may include low mood, loss of energy, changes in appetite and sleep patterns, difficulty concentrating, feelings of worthlessness or guilt, and in severe cases, thoughts of suicide. Depression can be caused by a variety of factors, including genetics, life events, brain chemistry, and other medical conditions. It is a treatable condition with a range of effective therapies, including medication, psychotherapy, and lifestyle changes.

Sadness and depression are different experiences. Feelings of sadness can be intense at times, but a person should still have moments of comfort or laughter. Sadness is a normal human response to challenges, setbacks, or losses. It can dissipate over time, allowing an individual to resume their daily life.

Lack of big emotions occurs when the ADHD brain feels like it doesn't have a source of stimulation. Our dopamine-seeking

79

For Parents

Want to help your child avoid emotional errors?

1. **Model good emotional management.** Which errors do you tend to make? Children learn by modeling what their parents are doing, not saying. Share your own emotions in a healthy way by saying, "I feel sad that we can't visit Grandma today," or "I'm surprised by the mean behavior of those boys at recess."
2. **Teach your child about emotions.** Help your child to recognize and define how they are feeling. When they learn that things that may seem amorphous or overwhelming actually have a name, they are empowered to manage them. Engage your child in conversations about feelings by discussing characters in books or TV shows. Occasionally, ask questions like, "How do you think this character feels?" With practice, your child's ability to identify their emotions will improve.
3. **Show acceptance.** It's okay to feel confused or overwhelmed. Acknowledge that your child is working through emotions, and that's perfectly fine. Crying, getting angry, and experiencing frustration are not signs of flaws or something to be fixed.

brains can drive us to scan our environment for engaging motivation, and when we don't find it, we are left wondering what is wrong with us.

Patrick was feeling gloomy. He couldn't figure out why he was not excited about anything. When I asked him about his home and work life, he talked about how he had to write an extensive white paper for his company that required exhaustive research. He had been working on this project for eight months without end. "It's a never-ending quest," he explained. There wasn't any dopamine to be found in his piles of research. In this case, Patrick

4. **Validate and relate.** Avoid minimizing your child's feelings. Saying "Stop getting so upset; it's not a big deal" may convey that their feelings are wrong. Validate their emotions, even if you think they appear disproportionate. Name the feeling and demonstrate understanding. Instead of saying, "I know you're mad we aren't going to the park today," say, "I know you're upset we aren't going to the park today. I get angry when I don't get to do things I want to do too." This reassures your child that everyone experiences these emotions, even if not as frequently or intensely.

5. **Separate feelings and behaviors.** Children should understand how to express their emotions in socially acceptable ways. Acting out in public, like screaming in a grocery store or throwing a tantrum at school, is not acceptable. Let them know it's okay to feel angry or scared but emphasize that they have choices in how they respond to these emotions. While they can be mad at someone, it doesn't justify hitting them. Similarly, feeling upset about a store being out of their favorite ice cream doesn't give them the right to throw a disruptive tantrum.

   Discipline behavior, not emotions. For instance, say, "You are going to time-out because you hit your brother," or, "You are losing this toy for the rest of the day because you are screaming, and it hurts my ears."

wasn't depressed or sad; his job had become tedious and boring with no end in sight.

We can also make this error when we lack inspiration or anticipation. Akeem asked, "Why do I get depressed after vacation?" I asked him what he meant, and he sighed. "I have nothing to look forward to anymore." He had looked forward to his trip to Portugal and used it as motivation to go to work every day. Now that his trip was over and he'd returned to the routine and responsibilities of daily life, he felt a lack of motivation, fatigue, and difficulty concentrating. His mind searched for excitement and

Avoid Reinforcing Emotional Errors

Sometimes parents inadvertently encourage their children's emotional errors. If you're working on helping your child regulate their emotions better, it's best to avoid the following:

1. **Rewarding your child for calming down.** If you offer your child a special treat every time they pull themselves together, they may learn that bursting into tears or yelling at their sibling is a good way to get something they want.
2. **Showering your child with attention during high emotional times.** While offering comfort is essential, ensure you don't overdo it. You don't want your child to learn that getting upset is the best strategy for attracting attention.
3. **Calming down your child constantly.** It's helpful to offer reassurance, but it's also important to teach your child the skills they will need to calm themselves down so they can handle their emotions when you're not there to step in and help.
4. **Telling your child to stop crying.** This might make them more upset. And if they see you getting worked up over their tears, they may think they're doing something wrong, which won't make it any easier to stop crying.

couldn't find any because he had no immediate plans for enjoyable or exciting activities.

Our emotions, although invaluable, can occasionally steer us astray. Classifying common emotional errors provides us with a powerful instrument for enhancing ourselves and nurturing personal growth.

As you read the five emotional errors, which ones did you see yourself making on a regular basis? You may have been taught

5. **Arguing with your child over emotions.** Engaging in arguments can exacerbate emotional tensions and invertedly teach emotional errors. It's essential to model constructive communication rather than getting into confrontations with your child. Encourage open dialogue and problem-solving instead of contributing to emotional turmoil.

For Your Personal Growth

Do you want to develop your own emotional resilience?

1. Pinpoint the specific errors you commonly make.
2. Seek support from close friends or family to recognize these emotional missteps.
3. When approaching those people, be explicit in your request. For example, say, "I've noticed a tendency to attribute my feelings to others. Can you please alert me when you observe me making this mistake?" Some individuals prefer using a designated code word, such as "bananas," as a gentle reminder for you to assess your emotions.
4. Remember that you invited others' feedback. Refrain from arguing; instead, attentively listen and express gratitude for their input.

these emotional patterns by your family, or you may have adopted them to navigate life's challenges. Choose one to work on. Make a point of catching it whenever you can. Ask a family member to help you identify when you make this error.

6

YOUR NERVOUS SYSTEM ISN'T BROKEN

'm going to be sick," I announced in our crowded cab. "I'm not joking," I added urgently. My always-prepared friend threw a gallon-sized Ziploc bag in my direction. Our taxi was in Dallas stop-and-go rush hour traffic, and I had food poisoning. I continued to make Jurassic-sounding roars for about forty-five minutes, only vaguely aware of how uncomfortable my three colleagues sharing the ride with me were. Only afterward, when my body was shaking from the intensity of the experience, was I embarrassed. It wasn't an ideal way to begin a tightly packed schedule of conference activities. Still, I pushed on, not considering that my nervous system had been challenged.

Three days later, I was headed back to the airport to catch an evening flight home, weary from a lack of sleep and high-carbohydrate hotel food. My nervous system still felt off from my ill-fated taxi ride. If everything went as planned, I would sleep on the plane, arrive home, experience a good night's sleep, and return to the airport the next morning feeling refreshed and ready to leave on my vacation to Spain.

While I was waiting to board the plane home, the flight attendant announced that the flight had been delayed and urged us to be patient. I glanced at my watch, calculating travel time and time zone differences. *That's okay*, I thought. *I still have time to catch my flight to Spain.*

Every two hours or so, we received an update reassuring passengers that they were working hard, but it would be a little longer. I glanced at my watch again. I began coaching myself. *Okay, you are tired. Stay calm and keep problem-solving. Keep your body calm. Breathe.* I also encouraged myself, *Stay in the mental game. Don't give in to anxiousness.* Though I was tired from the conference, I knew I needed to push through.

While I waited to board my plane, I strategized with my husband, who was at home, about how I could still make my flight to Spain. *That's good. Be a problem-solver, Tam. Good work,* I coached myself.

Twenty hours later, I was still in Dallas. I would need to rebook my ticket to Spain. I grumbled at the exorbitant rate but comforted myself. *You are making the best decisions with the information you have.* Although sad, I accepted that I would meet my daughter and friend in Spain a day later than planned.

When I finally boarded the plane in Dallas, I sank into my aisle seat, put my head in my hands, and felt the emotions I had been suppressing surge. I wasn't just crying; I was sobbing.

A flight attendant knelt beside me and asked, "Are you okay?" I answered in the garbled speech of someone who can't breathe, cry, and speak simultaneously. "I'll bring you some water," she said.

I had done my best to manage my emotions and to make decisions, but it came at a cost. My nervous system had been on high alert for a long time. My resilience was already low due to the food poisoning escapade. This was the letdown.

Little did I know this was only the beginning of a series of unfortunate events. During the next ten days on my vacation, my nervous system would be challenged in new ways: my brand-new phone would be stolen, I would experience a severe asthma attack and develop bronchitis, and I would visit an emergency room in the middle of the night to be diagnosed with COVID-19. This vacation was destined to teach me to observe and care for my nervous system.

Understanding the intricacies of ADHD involves examining its influence on our nervous system. People with ADHD have brains with different wiring than their peers who don't have ADHD. Dr. William Dodson, a psychiatrist with a specialty in ADHD, emphasizes the need to recognize those individuals as having a distinct type of nervous system. He asserts that while neurotypical individuals operate on an *importance-based* nervous system, those with ADHD navigate the world with an *interest-based* nervous system.[1] The interest-based system looks for dangers and exciting possibilities—and it can be exhausting because those of us with ADHD aren't deficient in attention. Instead, we pay attention to many sensory inputs while constantly monitoring our internal conversations. We usually have four or five things rattling around in our minds, like five monkeys talking to us simultaneously.

We experience unique challenges when it comes to our nervous system—our energy expenditure throughout the day is significant. Those of us with ADHD utilize our brain's energy differently. Our brain's battery depletes more rapidly, often resulting in a low-battery notification by late afternoon or even midmorning. Each time an executive function is employed and continuously utilized, it further drains the battery, leaving us feeling depleted. Russell Barkley, an expert on ADHD, explains that the energy consumed by our brains is a limited resource that needs replenishing to sustain our functioning.[2]

In addition to the cognitive drain, we also experience the physiological drain. Because of our quickly depleted mental battery, we tend to respond to situations with heightened stress as though we are responding to danger. As we respond with our fight, flight, freeze, or appease modes, we tend to experience more cortisol, adrenaline, and activation of the stress response system throughout our days. Because those of us with ADHD are extremely sensitive to our environments, we are constantly reading and responding to those environments.[3]

My trip to Dallas began with an assault on my nervous system in that taxi. From that event on, my ADHD nervous system was rarely at rest. Although the new environment and social interactions at the conference were engaging, interesting, and challenging, they were exhausting to my nervous system. My mind and body were on alert during the entire conference. And like many of my clients, I hadn't fully appreciated how fragile my nervous system is. Respecting this fact has helped me better manage my ADHD.

Importance-Based vs. Interest-Based Nervous Systems

Neurotypical people with importance-based nervous systems accomplish a task because it is somehow classified as significant. It may be classified as important. It could be personally meaningful or significant to them because it's important to someone else. Or the project may be important because there's a reward or consequence that comes from doing (or not doing) it. As one with ADHD, that's all I can tell you about this system. Many people without ADHD just seem to know what to do, when to do it, and how to do it. Their prefrontal cortex activity looks like wizardry to me.

If someone with an importance-based nervous system sees that the kitchen needs to be cleaned, they will probably do it because the kitchen ought to be cleaned. I watched as my college-age, non-ADHD daughter took out the trash this morning. I looked up from my work and thanked her. I knew the trash can was full because I had just opened the cabinet door to throw away the wrapper from my breakfast bar. But I had my mind on other things as I worked on my laptop at the dining room table. Her importance system approached it matter-of-factly. "It was full and needed to be taken out because it will overflow," she said when she opened the door to the garage and delivered the bag to the trash bin. According to Dodson, people with this type of nervous system drive action by assessing outcomes, rewards, and consequences. My daughter assessed the situation easily: the can would overflow and create a mess if more was placed in it.

On the other hand, I have an interest-based nervous system that isn't motivated by the theoretical importance of emptying the garbage can. I was thinking about the work I had to do today and was eager to start on that. Those of us with this type of nervous system are motivated by our interest in or passion for a task. In fact, I was irritated at the thought of the garbage can being full as I jammed the breakfast bar wrapper into it. Thinking that I *should* take out the trash isn't motivating enough for me to do it. For the most part, those of us with this nervous system are not motivated by importance, reward, or punishment. Instead, we need a genuine or intrinsic interest in the task or topic to muster the impulse to begin. I was interested in writing today, so the trash had to wait.

Dodson breaks this type of nervous system into five main factors that motivate action: interest, challenge, novelty, urgency, and passion. When one or more of these conditions is met, motivation comes easily to a person with ADHD, and the task is accomplished with single-mindedness. "It is a nervous system that works well using its own rules," Dodson explains.[4]

Those with an interest-based nervous system need one of these things to be activated:

- Interest or passion (a strong interest in a task or subject matter)
- Challenge or competition (competition against someone or a game of some sort)
- Novelty (a new gadget, routine, or strategy)

When we are "in the zone," we can cruise through a task with few impairments or executive function deficits. The downside of having this type of nervous system is that it is more sensitive to its environment and becomes easily depleted and exhausted.

The Window of Tolerance

One way of understanding ourselves and helping our nervous system is understanding our window of tolerance. In his book *The Developing Mind*, Dan Siegel describes the window of tolerance as a range of intensities of emotions that people can comfortably experience, process, and integrate.[5] Others have called it the "optimum arousal."[6] The window of tolerance is the zone where intense emotions and stress can be adapted to and processed in healthy ways.

Some people's window of tolerance is relatively wide. They can feel comfortable despite relatively high degrees of emotional intensity and tolerate a broad range of emotions, from pleasant ones such as excitement and happiness to unpleasant ones such as guilt or anger. When in this window of tolerance, they can react to stress, anxiety, and intense emotions effectively. The capacity to deal with stress in this space allows them to respond to the demands and pressures of everyday life without too much strain. When in their window of tolerance, they feel grounded, calm, and capable of accessing their intuition and rational mind.

How do you feel when you are in your window of tolerance? What are your thoughts? How do you act?

Everyone's window of tolerance—or zone of optimal arousal— has an upper and a lower boundary. As you can see from the window of tolerance diagram (image 6.1), above the upper boundary is the zone of hyperarousal, and below the lower boundary is the zone of hypoarousal. Many of us with ADHD have a less flexible nervous system, translating into a smaller window of tolerance. Daily events can frustrate our nervous system, and we find ourselves outside of the window. My nervous system was assaulted

(I'm sure my fellow travelers' systems were also) while I was in the taxi, placing me outside my window of tolerance. For the entire conference, I felt on high alert and unable to fully calm down. Instead of being calm and present, I was in hyperarousal.

Many of us with ADHD spend so much time outside our window of tolerance that we may not be able to remember what the window feels like. Thirty-year-old Kristine says she feels good in her skin when she's in her window of tolerance. "I mean, I'm who I want to be. Somehow I'm relaxed and alert at the same time— but it's totally balanced!" Many of my clients describe feeling energetic, creative, calm, happy, peaceful, and mellow. Kristine explains, "I find myself thinking, 'Hey, I've got this.'" In the window of tolerance, people tell me that they feel energetic, centered, grounded, fully engaged in life—and most of all, safe.

Take a moment to identify what your window of tolerance looks like. How do you feel when you are in it? What are your thoughts? How do you act?

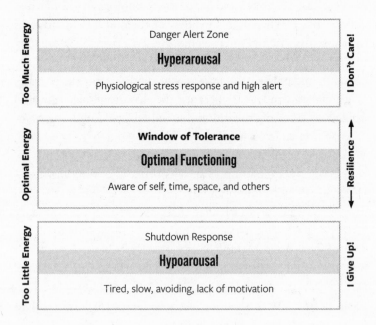

Hyperarousal

When we find ourselves in a state of hyperarousal, our bodies and minds undergo a profound transformation. It's as if a sudden alarm has gone off, urging us to focus on a perceived threat—the looming geometry test, an impending project deadline, or a loved one's stress. During these moments, our heart races, our eyes dart restlessly, and our entire being gears up for action, ready to fight, flee, freeze, or appease. It's a heightened state of reactivity and anxiety, where rapid thoughts and emotions overwhelm us, all driven by a single, primal goal: to alleviate that overwhelming discomfort.

It's important to emphasize that hyperarousal isn't inherently good or bad in the context of the stress response. Instead, it's a natural physiological and psychological reaction to stress or perceived danger. Hyperarousal can be beneficial in some situations, as it prepares our bodies for action and equips us to respond effectively to threats. Stress hormones like adrenaline and cortisol are released, enhancing our alertness, focus, and physical readiness.

Yet when hyperarousal spirals beyond our window of tolerance, it can engulf our minds, temporarily disabling rational thinking and social behavior. Some may refer to this as "amygdala hijacking" or "emotional flooding."

In the modern era, hyperarousal is a challenge because our stressors may not involve life-and-death situations, but they often feel urgent and relentless. The demands of work, bills, and financial pressures create persistent and prolonged stressors. For those of us with ADHD, hyperarousal can become a daily occurrence, a constant companion.

After a bout of hyperarousal, excess emotions are released, returning the body to its window of tolerance and completing the stress cycle. It's akin to letting out a long-held breath, restoring balance to the nervous system. I recall the moment at the Dallas airport when I sensed that I had pushed myself to the upper limit of my window. I tried to regain control by employing my emotional protocol—self-coaching, deep breathing, and slowing down my thoughts. However, the hours at the airport took their toll, and I eventually slipped into hyperarousal. Stress surged through me as I attempted to think of ways to get home and then to be able to go on vacation. Once I was safely on the plane, I could no longer contain my feelings. The dam burst, letting all the excess energy out. As I ugly-cried, I felt my body discharge anxiety, fear, and the energy that hyperarousal had built up. Once I had finished, I napped like an exhausted toddler after a day at the park.

Releasing excess energy is necessary to restore the nervous system to the window of tolerance. Sometimes, though, we fail to complete the stress cycle. Our innate hyperarousal response activates to protect us from perceived threats. We are unaware when the danger dissipates, and we remain locked in a heightened sense of alertness. Many clients begin their sessions in such a hyperaroused state, their bodies tense, eyes darting as they hastily recount their overwhelming experiences.

"Your nervous system is overwhelmed," I often observe, which typically elicits puzzled looks. Many people are unaware that they consider a state of hyperarousal their normal baseline. Before we can address what to do for their nervous system, they need to be able to identify when they are outside their window of tolerance.

Sadie, a computer programmer in her thirties, shared that she felt irritable and agitated during hyperarousal. "It's like I'm mad at everyone and everything." Although her thoughts were hard to pin down during these moments, she eventually said, "I guess I just want to make it stop." On the other hand, her behaviors were clear to her because they landed her on a performance improvement plan at work. "I'm told that I just start yelling at people."

"Do you yell?" I asked.

"Well, yes," she admitted, then quickly added, "I'm just trying to get stuff done." Snapping at her coworkers was her unconscious attempt to make the hyperarousal stop. It's an uncomfortable state, and like Sadie, many of us desperately want it to end,

HYPERAROUSAL = too much energy
HYPOAROUSAL = too little energy

often resorting to actions that we believe will provide relief, even if it means yelling or fighting to feel better.

Not all of us yell and get angry like Sadie. Sometimes it feels like the volume control on our five senses is turned up too high. We may become jumpy and easily startled by sounds. Or we suddenly feel like our shoes are too tight. Our thoughts will also seem to race and swirl around. When our level of arousal moves beyond the limits of our window of tolerance, a deluge of energy blasts our mind and takes over several processes like rational thinking and social behavior.

For those of us with ADHD, it seems that we are drawn into hyperarousal as a way of engaging with our environment. Our brains constantly look for any hint of challenge, novelty, urgency, or passion. Even something that's not a threat can become intriguing and, consequently, a potential source of stress. It doesn't help that some of us will intentionally use hyperarousal to kick-start progress toward accomplishing a task. Because our interest-based nervous systems remain alert to our surroundings, we often feel drained and tired.

Take a moment to recognize what hyperarousal looks like for you. How do you feel when you're in it? What thoughts occupy your mind? How do you behave? If you're unsure, ask friends and family for their insights—hyperarousal tends to be quite apparent to those around us. Recognizing what hyperarousal looks like for you is a crucial step in understanding and managing this pervasive aspect of our human experience.

Hypoarousal

Hypoarousal, the counterpart to hyperarousal, often remains in the shadows when we think of stress responses. While we commonly associate stress with the fight-or-flight reaction, our bodies can just as readily respond by freezing or appeasing when they sense excessive pressure or "charge." These hypoaroused states serve as a protective mechanism, slowing us down to prevent overwhelm. When we're in a hypoaroused condition, we might exhibit low energy, sluggishness, reduced alertness, and a decreased responsiveness to stimuli.

Hypoarousal can manifest as a natural response to tiredness or sleep deprivation. When our bodies lack adequate rest or sleep, they enter a state of reduced arousal, leading to feelings of fatigue, drowsiness, and diminished mental and physical performance. In the context of trauma, hypoarousal can act as a safeguard. During or after a traumatic event, the body and mind may become hypoaroused to cope and self-preserve. This response helps us distance ourselves emotionally and sensory-wise from the overwhelming experience.

For many of us with ADHD, hypoarousal often surfaces when we are overstimulated. Our natural inclination is to dull our senses. This can make us feel heavy, tired, and foggy. Interestingly, research suggests that those with ADHD who have nervous system dysregulation are more likely to encounter hypoarousal. This is especially true with tasks such as planning, organizing, time management, and emotional regulation.[7]

"It's like I am glued to my phone," seventeen-year-old Beckett told me. "I'm lying on my bed, scrolling, and a part of me knows that I should be doing something else, but I'm in a trance." Other clients describe this as feeling foggy, lethargic, low in energy, or fatigued. Beckett explains that his only thought is to disconnect

Having a narrow window of tolerance makes it more challenging to navigate stressors effectively.

Making Connections

For those of you who read my first book, *Your Brain's Not Broken*, hyperarousal describes the Red Quadrant on the Solve-It Grid. Hypoarousal describes the Blue Quadrant.

and to stay disconnected. When I asked him what caused his hypoaroused response, he shrugged and said, "Everything. It all feels too big." Then he added, "School, mostly."

We all have our moments of downshifting. After a few hours of shopping, my non-ADHD friend plans our next assault on a store, saying, "I think we should look at . . ." Meanwhile, I stare at nothing and nod. I just want to nap. Shopping is an arduous activity for me. She recognizes my hypoarousal and says, "Let's take a break and get some food." By the end of our early lunch, I have returned to my talkative self, and we can go to another store. Hypoarousal exists on a spectrum, ranging from mild experiences triggered by sensory overload or specific situations to complete immobilization in cases of extreme trauma.

Sometimes my clients talk about feeling depressed. Although depression is a form of hypoarousal, they are usually talking about a recurring feeling of ADHD-related hypoarousal. That feeling is typically connected to a specific activity or subject, like work. It occurs for a shorter time, and they are unable to upshift from this state. For example, if you must set up a series of meetings with various stakeholders for your company that seem unnecessary, your interest-based nervous system may not be activated, preventing you from having the energy or motivation to approach the stakeholders. In hypoarousal, you feel apathetic toward the task and have little fuel to act. Depression, however, is longer lasting and affects all areas of your life. Activities that once brought you

Putting It into Practice

For many of us, managing mornings can be challenging, causing us to rev up our nervous system into hyperarousal. Incorporating specific strategies can help make the mornings more manageable and help us remain within our window of tolerance. Here are some tips:

1. **Think about your future self.** Wouldn't it be great if you woke up to find that your "past self" had laid out your clothes, packed your bag, and ensured everything you needed for the next day was ready the night before? Wouldn't you be so grateful? The night before a big day, think about your "future self" and how to help him or her have a great morning. A client recently told me, "I love when my past self makes overnight oats for me! I can have a fast, healthy breakfast. I am so proud of him!"

2. **Leave yourself a note the night before.** Create visual schedules or checklists to help guide you through your morning routine. Visual aids can serve as reminders for tasks you need to complete. It could be setting things together on a counter, a short list, or even a nice note, like "Dear Morning Tamara, before you leave today, you need to remember to turn off the porch light, take the trash to the curb, and feed the cat."

3. **The floor-is-hot-lava approach.** Use alarms or timers to keep you on track. Set reminders to start a new task or move on to the

joy now feel dull. If you are very unclear about which one you are experiencing, please see an ADHD-informed therapist to help you distinguish between the two.

In my personal journey, as I began monitoring my own nervous system, I was surprised by how frequently I experienced both hyper- and hypoarousal and how long it took to return to my window of tolerance. It's worth noting that individuals with ADHD tend to have more rigid nervous systems. We not only find it easier next step in your routine. For example, an alarm can remind you to move from the bathroom to the kitchen. The catch is that once you leave the bathroom, the floor turns into hot lava, and you must avoid returning.

Although many of my clients use this strategy with their children, it's not just a parenting strategy. I use it frequently because it engages my imagination and keeps me out of hyperarousal. If I need to return to my bedroom to retrieve an item, I say aloud, "Hot lava, hot lava, hot lava." It's a silly thing that helps me avoid the otherwise inevitable distractions I could encounter while staying in a relaxed, playful state.

4. **Remember that it always takes longer than you think.** Many of us with ADHD are notoriously time blind. One aspect of this disadvantage is our inability to estimate how long things will take. Build in extra time for unexpected delays or distractions. Having a buffer can reduce stress and prevent a sense of rush.

5. **Life-should-have-a-soundtrack strategy.** One of my clients has a playlist for managing her mornings. She listens to Taylor Swift while putting on her makeup and doing her hair. Then, when Bruno Mars sings, she transitions to the kitchen to get breakfast. She told me how she remembers her cues: "Taylor helps me get ready, and then I eat breakfast with Bruno."

What can you do to avoid starting your day in hyperarousal?

to move out of our window of tolerance, which is often smaller to begin with, but we also take longer to return to it after experiencing stress. Understanding these nuances is crucial in managing our responses to stress and maintaining our well-being.

Our ADHD nervous systems aren't broken; they simply struggle with handling the various challenges and fluctuations that life throws our way. Learning about our window of tolerance and how to expand it can significantly enhance our ability to navigate these ups and downs effectively. As we increase our self-awareness and resilience, we can identify the times when we are out of our window.

The next chapter explores specific strategies and practices for expanding and optimizing our window of tolerance, further enhancing our capacity to thrive in the face of life's challenges.

7

WIDENING THE WINDOW

In the previous chapter, we learned about the window of tolerance, a state of emotional and physiological balance where we can effectively manage stress and cope with life's challenges. This is the comfortable range within which we can experience many emotions without becoming overwhelmed or dysregulated. We can think clearly, make rational decisions, and engage in healthy relationships within our window of tolerance. However, during times of excessive stress, the window of tolerance can shrink, causing us to become either hyperaroused, characterized by anxiety, anger, or panic, or hypoaroused, marked by dissociation or emotional numbing. Our goal is to expand our window of tolerance, allowing us to navigate life's ups and downs with greater resilience and emotional stability.

Expanding your window of tolerance involves two essential steps for improving your ability to handle a broader range of emotional states and stressors. The first step is to enhance your awareness of your nervous system's signals. Pay attention to how your body and mind react in order to recognize when you're in a state of hyperarousal (overstimulated) or hypoarousal (understimulated). The second step is learning how to handle your nervous system better,

A key to effectively managing your nervous system lies in getting comfortable with discomfort.

especially when dealing with discomfort. When you're in the middle of strong emotional reactions, it can be challenging to remember that these feelings won't last forever. But it's helpful to remind yourself that they will eventually go away. You can also develop ways to cope with these problematic sensations and emotions, making you feel better once those uncomfortable feelings fade.

You can actively intervene to shift the state of your nervous system. Learn what it feels like to be outside your window and identify your stress in terms of a hypo or hyper state. Keep track of a few telltale signs that you're outside your window. Maybe you notice your breathing picks up or you feel tension in your stomach. Perhaps you start to feel numb or disconnected from yourself. Understanding your own patterns will help you figure out what to do next.

Upregulation and downregulation are fundamental aspects of managing your nervous system. Upregulation involves techniques and practices that activate and energize your nervous system, heightening your alertness and readiness to face challenges. Downregulation, conversely, focuses on methods that calm and soothe your nervous system, enabling you to release tension, alleviate stress, and restore a sense of tranquility. As we explore upregulation and downregulation, you will discover the valuable tools necessary to fine-tune your nervous system and achieve a balance that promotes a wider window of tolerance.

Upregulation

Before my clients choose activities to energize their nervous system, I ask them to share a metaphor for how they feel when in hypoarousal. Amari told me that when she feels hypoaroused, it's like trying to light a damp matchstick on a rainy day. She envisioned striving to create a spark and was frustrated when nothing happened. She felt this way when she knew she should begin a task.

Jay described his hypoaroused state differently. "It's like my brain has decided to take a vacation in a hammock, sipping on a margarita with a tiny umbrella, while the rest of my body is trying to direct a middle school play without any rehearsals." For him, hypoarousal felt like his brain and body weren't connected.

When I am in a hypoaroused state, my brain feels slow, like it is trudging through knee-deep mud while wearing lead boots. *Schlurp!* I can almost hear the sucking sounds a boot makes as you pull it out of the mucky mess and attempt to step forward. Every thought and movement seems heavy and burdensome. When I imagine hearing that schlurping sound, I know it is time to find a strategy to upregulate.

Describing your feelings in a hypoaroused state can help you identify more easily when you are in it. Your metaphor can also help you determine which activity may work best for you.

There are many strategies to choose from when addressing your hypoarousal. Several breathwork exercises aim to energize. The Wim Hof Method, the "breath of fire" method, and the 5-3-3 technique all have different applications and benefits. You can read about these techniques online and select the ones that work best for you.

Amari uses the 5-3-3 technique to address her wet-match scenario. First, she takes five deep breaths, inhaling through her nose

When in hypoarousal, use upregulating strategies. When in hyperarousal, use downregulating strategies.

and exhaling out her mouth to completely fill and then empty her lungs. Then she takes three fast breaths, inhaling through her nose and pushing her breath out on the exhale through her mouth. Finally, she takes three loud breaths, inhaling through her nose and releasing loudly with sound out of her mouth. She repeats this process until she feels energized.

Jay uses physical activity to bring his brain back from vacation. When he feels like he is in hypoarousal, he does wall push-ups and a two-minute plank. "My office mates have gotten used to seeing me on the floor in an isometric hold," he says with a laugh. He returns to work with his brain and body reconnected.

You could try going for a brisk walk, doing some jumping jacks, or engaging in your favorite form of exercise. Even a short burst of movement can make a big difference.

Although it sounds counterintuitive, when I hear my metaphorical leaden boots slogging through the mud, I know I need a power nap. A ten- to twenty-minute nap refreshes my mind and provides a quick energy boost without making me groggy. I keep a small pillow and blanket in my office for that energy boost. During my break on those long days at the office, I lie on the floor and calm my body—and yes, I've trained myself to snooze for a few minutes. (Caveat: You need to have had a good night's sleep to power nap. If your body and brain are hungry for rest, this strategy could backfire and make you drowsier.)

Getting out of a hypoaroused state can be challenging. Still, you can try several activities to help increase your energy and alertness. Remember to set timers so that you know when to return to your work. Here are some ideas:

1. *Splash cold water on yourself.* A quick splash on your face or hands can invigorate you and wake you up.
2. *Listen to uplifting music.* Put on your favorite high-energy music and have a mini dance party, or simply let the music energize you.

3. *Engage in mindful meditation.* While this might sound counterintuitive, engaging in a short mindfulness or meditation session can help increase your awareness and focus, helping you snap out of hypoarousal.

4. *Drink water.* Dehydration can lead to fatigue, so ensure you're adequately hydrated throughout the day.

5. *Socialize.* Interacting with friends or coworkers can stimulate your mind and provide a mental boost.

6. *Change your environment.* Sometimes a change of scenery can do wonders. Step outside for a breath of fresh air or move to a different room if you're indoors.

7. *Eat a healthy snack.* Healthy snacks like fruits, nuts, or yogurt can provide a quick energy boost.

8. *Laugh.* Watch a funny video or read a joke to bring laughter into your day. Laughter releases endorphins, which can improve your mood and energy levels.

Remember that everyone's response to these activities may vary, so find what works best for you. If you find yourself frequently experiencing hypoarousal or extreme fatigue, it's a good idea to consult a health care professional to rule out any underlying medical issues.

Downregulation

Just as I do with hypoarousal, I ask my clients to describe how they feel when they are hyperaroused. Jay described his hyperarousal this way: "I feel like I'm multitasking like a caffeinated octopus, answering emails, making phone calls, and juggling office supplies simultaneously." His attempts at multitasking made him less efficient.

Amari described her hyperarousal differently. "I feel tense, like I'm running away from spies, and yet somehow, I manage to trip over my shoelaces. I hurry to get up because the spies are still chasing me." She described some anxiety and mental clumsiness that she felt while hyperaroused.

For me, hyperarousal feels like I'm playing a game of Tetris. Chores, responsibilities, and routines fall from the top of the screen in various shapes like T, L, and Z, and I try to manipulate them as they fall. I try to arrange them so they fit neatly together, forming complete lines without gaps. Like in the game, the objects fall faster and faster, forcing me to react even more quickly. Out of determination and desperation, I slam pieces into place, hoping for the line-clearing combo. For a long time, I thought my hyperaroused Tetris approach was the only way to accomplish anything.

When Jay senses that the caffeinated octopus has been occupying his office, he uses a technique called progressive muscle relaxation. Sitting in his office chair, he tenses and then relaxes each muscle group in his body. "I start with my toes and work my way up to my head," he says. He hadn't noticed how tense his muscles were while his keyboard clicked like a machine gun and his mouse moved faster than a hummingbird's wings. "By the time I'm finished, I feel like I'm relaxed and able to think clearly again."

Amari uses breathwork to downregulate because it is the quickest way to eliminate the "spies" chasing her. Though many options for breathwork promote relaxation, Amari decided to keep it simple. She sits up straight and inhales through her nose while expanding her abdomen and chest. Then she exhales completely through her mouth. While doing that, she concentrates only on the airflow from her nose, lungs, and belly and back through her mouth. "You hear people say, 'Just breathe' like it's some sort of a cliché, but it really is so effective," Amari says.

I've learned to turn to tapping to address my emotional distress and regulate my nervous system. Tapping, or emotional freedom technique, is a psychological acupressure method that involves tapping specific points on the body with the fingertips. Tapping these energy meridian points can help restore balance and alleviate emotional discomfort. I was reluctant and skeptical to try tapping, but after reading the impressive research, I'm glad I tried it.

Downregulating your nervous system involves activities and practices that help calm and soothe your body and mind. These techniques are especially beneficial when you're feeling stressed, anxious, or overwhelmed.

1. *Listen to soothing music.* Play calming music or sounds, such as nature sounds or instrumental music, to help relax your mind.

2. *Use aromatherapy.* Certain scents, like lavender or frankincense, are known for their calming effects. Use essential oils or scented candles to create a relaxing atmosphere.

3. *Journal.* Journaling offers another powerful avenue for interpreting your nervous system's signals. Some clients have calmed themselves down by using this peculiar prompt: write a dialogue between yourself and your nervous system. This can help you identify patterns and triggers that impact your well-being.

4. *Use coregulation with a loved one.* Do you have that person who helps you shift out of a dysregulated state? When you connect to a loved one who is in a regulated state through touch, breath, or verbal mirroring, you can regulate your nervous systems simultaneously. Research also suggests that dogs, cats, and rabbits have similar effects regulating our nervous systems.

5. *Try nature or forest bathing.* Forest bathing is the Japanese practice of relaxation where you simply walk among the trees, observing nature around you while breathing deeply. Going for a walk in nature has been shown to reduce stress markers considerably for anyone. Additionally, studies have found that spending time in green outdoor

settings, such as parks, gardens, or natural reserves, can offer a multisensory experience that can be calming and engaging.

6. *Use Epsom salt baths.* Many of my clients tell me that they love taking an Epsom salt bath to reset their nervous system. Not only does the magnesium in Epsom salt help relax your muscles, but it can also help relax your mind. Research has shown that magnesium deficiency enhances stress reactions, and utilizing the healing properties of soaking in Epsom salt can help reduce stress and cortisol levels.

7. *Rest and relax without screen time or obligations.* I love my screens as much as the next person, but I try to have at least a half hour a day without technology. While it can be hard to unplug, it's important to take some time for rest and relaxation without screens. Allowing your body time to relax is crucial in strengthening the nervous system.

8. *Weigh yourself down.* Many of my clients soothe their system by adding a bit of weight. No, I don't mean body weight, so don't hit the Oreos in the pantry. Using weighted blankets, resting a backpack full of books on your legs, or even pushing a lawn mower are ways to provide your brain with proprioception—sensory infor- mation the body receives from the specialized receptors in muscles, tendons, joints, and other connective tissues. These can produce a calming and organizing effect on your nervous system.

Remember that different techniques work for different people, so find what resonates with you and practice it regularly to man- age hyperarousal effectively. Seeking professional guidance can be invaluable if you find it challenging to manage high arousal levels independently.

Need Help Staying in the Window of Tolerance?

Some studies suggest that listening to baroque music, which is known for its structured and ornate style, might have a positive effect on people with ADHD. Baroque music, like compositions by Bach or Vivaldi, has a steady rhythm and predictable patterns that could help improve focus and attention.

These are my favorite compositions that I use to help me remain in my window of tolerance:

> *Brandenburg Concertos* by Johann Sebastian Bach
> *Water Music* by George Frideric Handel
> *The Four Seasons* by Antonio Vivaldi
> *Canon in D* by Johann Pachelbel
> *Violin Concerto in D Major* by Johannes Brahms

The ideal time to work on widening your window of tolerance is when you find yourself at the edges of it during moments of discomfort. Remember that you can't always control your initial reaction. Still, you can actively intervene to restore your nervous system balance. To do this, identify whether you're in a hypo or hyper state by recognizing telltale signs like breathing changes, body tension, or a sense of disconnection, or by referring to your metaphor. Then choose the appropriate upregulation or down-regulation activities. Consider working with a therapist or coach to learn and practice coping skills tailored to your needs, which will better support your return to baseline.

By intentionally moving your nervous system from a state of stress to one of safety, you enhance your ability to self-regulate. Keep a toolbox of these coping skills ready for when you need them. Having a variety of coping techniques at your disposal is helpful because not all strategies work equally well in every situation.

> **When you learn how to work within your window** of tolerance and expand it, you'll find it easier to return to a calm, rational, and capable baseline. Slowing breathwork is one of the fastest ways to activate the relaxation response.

Broadening my window of tolerance involves spending time in nature, practicing yin yoga, and savoring a pot of tea. These activities slow me down and increase my capacity to remain within my window, especially when I lean toward hyperarousal.

Family Nervous Systems

In family settings where ADHD is present, it's essential to acknowledge that when one member's nervous system is dysregulated, it can impact everyone. However, trying to accommodate one individual's dysregulation is not the solution. Each family member, from school-age children to adults, must learn how to manage their nervous system. You can, however, provide a calm presence that will help your loved ones return to their window of tolerance. The best thing you can do when someone around you is dysregulated is to manage *your* nervous system and remain in *your* own window.

> The best thing you can do when someone around you is dysregulated is to manage *your* nervous system and remain in *your* own window.

During my disastrous taxi ride described in chapter 6, a calm colleague sat beside me. She didn't ask me if I needed anything, probably because she knew I couldn't answer. Instead, she remained calm, not looking at me or drawing attention to my situation. She handed me tissues regularly and talked to the taxi driver, trying to get him to roll down the locked windows.

She was a calm presence for me. Then six days later, while I was struggling to breathe in Spain, my daughter calmly said, "I think we need to get you to a hospital." She was my hero, arranging for us to get to a hospital in the middle of the night in a foreign country. She didn't use many words. She didn't fuss over me, share her anxiety with me, or even rebuke me for not having an emergency inhaler. She remained calm and was able to lead my out-of-balance nervous system. These two individuals monitored their nervous systems and, as a result, helped me manage mine.

It Takes Time

Working on widening our window of tolerance takes time and effort. So many of us with ADHD neglect navigating our inner world because of the tyranny of daily tasks and an endless list of to-dos. When a doctor challenged me to use heart rate variability biofeedback to help me balance my nervous system, I instinctively responded, "Who has the time for that?" Then my mind sped to all the other healthy habits I should be doing like flossing my teeth, exercising, and drinking enough water. It seemed so overwhelming to do all the things I should be doing. But I reminded myself that my nervous system is critical for my healthy functioning and followed my doctor's suggestion.

Managing our nervous system promotes better management of our emotions. In the next chapter, we will examine two paths of thinking: survival and transformational. We'll think about how and when to maximize our time in transformational thinking and leave the survival thinking for actual calamities.

For Your Personal Growth

When working on widening your window of tolerance, engaging in self-reflection can be helpful. Here are some questions you may consider asking yourself:

1. **What are my typical stressors that seem to push me out of my window of tolerance?** Identify specific situations or triggers that commonly cause stress or discomfort for you.

2. **How do I currently cope with stress?** Do you tend to go to hyper-arousal or hypoarousal? Reflect on your current coping mechanisms and whether they are effective in helping you manage stressors.

3. **What is my metaphor for how I feel when I'm hyperaroused and when I'm hypoaroused? What physical sensations do I associate with each?** Use your metaphor to identify when you're approaching the edges of your window of tolerance. Pay attention to how stress manifests in your body.

4. **Do I have a support system in place?** Consider the strength of your social support network. Having people you can turn to for understanding and assistance can be crucial in expanding your window of tolerance.

5. **Am I practicing self-care regularly?** Assess your self-care practices. Are you prioritizing activities that promote physical and emotional well-being? Think of these activities as the window of tolerance training.

6. **What activities help me return to the window of tolerance?** Keep this list handy so that you can refer to it when you are out of your window of tolerance. Be willing to explore and learn new coping strategies through self-help resources or professional guidance.

Remember that self-reflection is an ongoing process. Revisit these questions periodically as you continue to widen your window of tolerance. If you need additional support, consider seeking guidance from a mental health professional.

8

PERILS OF THE TELEPHOTO LENS

When our brain senses that we are in grave danger, it naturally selects the telephoto lens to protect us. Long ago, on an early snowy morning, I was on my way to the high school where I taught part-time. My two young children were secured in their car seats and dozing when my SUV hit a thin coating of ice on the highway. My car spun in circles. I watched as a black car and then a truck passed by my spiraling car as if it were happening in slow motion. Instead of fear, I felt an unmistakable sensation of slowness. I watched my vehicle twirl like a slowing carnival ride, and the other cars around me continued in a straight line.

I looked out the driver's side window and saw a red car heading for the rear driver's side, where my daughter slept. Feeling helpless to avoid the collision, I looked back at my sweet-faced infant daughter. "I'm sorry," I whispered. I attempted to steer into the skid and away from the car. Suddenly, snow splashed against the windshield as my car skidded down the shallow ravine of southbound US 131 and stopped. Time suddenly returned to normal speed. My heart raced, and I checked the back seat. My nervous system and survival brain signaled that it was safe to respond.

My children were still quiet and seemed unconcerned about what we had just experienced. It had lasted only a few seconds but seemed much longer. Taking a deep breath, I put my car in four-wheel drive, slowly pulled out of the ditch, and backed onto the highway. The rest of the day, I tried to process what had happened.

I had experienced a Matrix-like moment. In the movie *The Matrix*, there is a scene where time slows down, and Neo, played by Keanu Reeves, bends backward to dodge bullets being shot at him by one of the villainous agents. That scene made cinematic history, using over one hundred cameras to make the illusion come to life.

Researchers believe our minds go into a mode of extreme speed in a dangerous situation, making it seem like what is happening in the outside world slows down.[1] As my nervous system upregulated to process the danger, so did my mental state. Since everything seemed to slow down in the environment, I saw and heard more details of what was happening, which led to the feeling that the event lasted longer than it did. After twenty-five years, I remember that moment like hundreds of individual telephotos taken within seconds. At that moment in the car, my only concern was for my children's and my own safety. I was at the center of all the action and didn't consider the impact on other drivers, my vehicle, and least of all, whether I would miss work. I was only concerned about survival. The brain's telephoto lens is intended to keep us safe.

What if you could use only a telephoto lens on a camera? Or only 2.5x zoom or higher on your phone? What would your photos look like? A telephoto lens magnifies your subject, capturing the minute detail of a particular topic or scene, and the background is blurred or missing.

One day, my daughter sent me a photo of a rodent she found floating in our pool. I was shocked. The image appeared to depict a large, ratlike creature. I had no idea we had animals that looked like that in our area. I asked, "Could you place it next to something for scale?" The following photo was of the animal in the pool skimmer, after it had been fished out and was lying on the pool deck beside the filter cover. Now, having perspective, I could see that it was a vole, a small animal that looked like a field mouse. Instead of the two-foot monstrosity I had expected, I could now see it was about four or five inches long. "It's still gross," my daughter said when I explained it.

Perspective is important. When we use only the telephoto lens, we miss essential contexts. Sometimes our thinking habits focus on the wrong things, and we lose perspective.

Misusing the Telephoto Lens

Although I had met with this parent before, his tsunami of emotions surprised me. Before I could ask my typical opening question, "What should we discuss today?" Nick began talking quickly and loudly. "I know you'll say that we need to focus on me and my parenting, but we need to get some things straightened out with Sam, or he's not returning to college." He told me the latest happenings and then said, "Oh, he says he's working on things with his ADHD coach, but you know him—he can be charming. He's probably fooling the coach. I told him he's not returning to college unless he . . ." Nick then shared a long list of behavioral demands. Finally, his seismic wave of emotions crested. "We've been fighting the whole time he's been on semester break. I tell him to do something, and he fights me. I am so sick of all this! I can't keep doing this!"

Family members can drive us bonkers. Sometimes the more we love them, the more irrational we feel. And for those of us who are parents, our physiological disposition makes it even more challenging to reason about our progeny. Everything in our body rejects calm, balanced thinking and screams, "Protect and fight for this child!" even if that means fighting *them*.

Nick had concerns not only about his son's academic performance but also about the kind of adult Sam would become. Nick's survival instincts kicked in, making him react like his son's life was in danger. "I've always been anxious about Sam," he admitted. "I care deeply for him but often get frustrated too." He also wondered if Sam would ever become a fully functioning adult. Nick couldn't think clearly enough to work through issues with his son. Instead, he felt the urge to impose a solution on him.

When we view our loved ones through a telephoto lens, we magnify the problems we see and lose sight of the bigger picture. In other words, we fail to consider the context and broader perspective. Out of a sense of love and fear, parents often find themselves in this unproductive place. In this heightened state, Nick couldn't stay calm and focus on finding solutions.

A problem arises when we sense danger that isn't truly dangerous in the modern world. The problem with using a telephoto lens, metaphorically at least, is that it blurs the background so we cannot see the entire landscape. Nick used his telephoto lens to examine Sam's life, especially his son's academic performance. He wasn't asking other questions like, *Is Sam emotionally healthy? How is he doing socially? Does he have friends with whom he can share his life? Does he remain hopeful about his future despite struggling at school? What does he think about his performance? Does he have a plan to improve? Does he understand the boundaries of our financial support?*

I asked Nick about the larger picture, and he said, "Sam's fine. He has too many friends, and that is distracting him. He's not trying hard enough. He should feel scared about his future because that's good for him. He says he has a plan, but I don't trust him." Nick felt he had all the information he needed, so he diagnosed Sam's problem and assumed he knew the correct answers. He was anxious about his son's success. Instead of owning that and working through his emotions, he focused only on Sam's academic life.

Using a telephoto lens at the wrong times leads to unhealthy egocentrism, where we focus only on what we see and feel in the moment.

Survival Thinking

Survival thinking is what happens when we rely on our telephoto lens. Our survival mindset is a cognitive and emotional state we enter when we perceive a situation as threatening our well-being or survival. In this state, the brain and body prioritize immediate survival over other considerations, such as rational decision-making or long-term planning. Nick narrowed his focus on his son's grades as the perceived threat while ignoring or downplaying additional information.

Fear, anger, and anxiety are heightened during survival thinking, making it difficult to remain calm and composed. In survival mode, rational thinking and problem-solving abilities can be impaired. The primary goal is to escape or eliminate the perceived threat.

We tend to look at life very narrowly when we slip into survival mode. We mainly think about how things affect us personally. We focus on our emotions and thoughts when we feel angry, rejected, disrespected, or hurt. We feel like we have to act on our strong opinions and feelings. When we have conflicts, we often blame others to make ourselves feel better. We try to make ourselves believe that we're the ones who've been mistreated and are victims.

Survival mode is an egocentric place. Our heightened self-awareness and self-focus make it hard to see the bigger picture. We assume everyone sees things like we do. It can be challenging to imagine other people having different perspectives.

The table near the end of this chapter shows a list of behaviors associated with survival thinking. Which ones do you see yourself using frequently?

Survival thinking can affect all adults, but it's particularly noticeable in people with ADHD. Sometimes those with ADHD may be seen as self-centered when trapped in survival thinking. "My wife gets mad at me when I don't ask her about her day or how she feels," Hudson, a thirty-one-year-old, shared. "How can I? I'm barely making it through my day. I'm surprised by how much time basic tasks take. I never feel like I'm getting it all done." Tasks that might seem easy for others, like grocery shopping, laundry, and arriving at work on time, aren't easy for Hudson. He responds to feeling overwhelmed by entering survival mode, acting like his chores and errands are a matter of life and death.

So many of us are just coping with daily life, hoping to get by, marching from one day to the next, and it is difficult to imagine anything different. Transformational thinking offers a more empowered mindset compared to survival thinking.

Transformational Thinking

Transformational thinking is like possessing various camera lenses, including ultra wide-angle, wide-angle, standard, macro, telephoto, and even super telephoto. Just as photographers use multiple lenses to adapt to different shooting scenarios, transformational thinkers use different lenses to navigate life's challenges, recognizing their ability to manage their emotions, thoughts, expectations, and judgments. As they become skilled at using different lenses, they adjust their perceptions, interpretations, and responses to those around them and life's circumstances.

Essential aspects of transformational thinking include:

- *Emotional autonomy.* Transformational thinkers can maintain emotional autonomy, meaning they are not overly swayed or controlled by the emotions of others. They can experience and express their feelings while remaining balanced and independent.
- *Personal identity.* Transformational thinkers have a strong sense of self and a clear understanding of their values, beliefs, and goals. They are less likely to conform to external pressures or societal expectations that may compromise their sense of identity.

- *Maintaining boundaries.* Transformational thinkers establish and maintain healthy emotional boundaries. They can distinguish between their own emotions and those of others.
- *Adaptability.* Transformational thinkers are more flexible to change and can navigate life's challenges with resilience. They make decisions based on their own principles rather than being overly influenced by external circumstances or the opinions of others.
- *Well-regulated empathy.* Transformational thinkers can empathize with others without losing their own identity or becoming entangled in others' emotional states. Chapter 16 discusses how to offer support without becoming overwhelmed or overly invested in the emotions of others.
- *Straightforward communication.* Transformational thinkers can express their thoughts and emotions clearly and listen attentively without being defensive or reactive.

Developing transformational thinking is a lifelong process and can lead to healthier family relationships and individual well-being. The table near the end of this chapter shows a list of behaviors associated with transformational thinking. Which ones do you see yourself using frequently?

We can learn more about transformational thinking by observing others who use it regularly. Look for people who are self-aware and purposeful in their actions. They know their beliefs and don't require others to agree. They take responsibility for their behaviors, emotions, and ADHD-related challenges, even offering appropriate apologies when acting from a survival mindset. While in their transformational mindset, they don't try to change you; instead, they accept you as you are, expecting you to take responsibility for your actions.

Look for individuals who are committed to personal growth and openly admit they're a work in progress. Being around them might make you feel more balanced and self-aware. Can you identify anyone in your family or community who embodies transformational thinking?

Transformational Thinking 101

Although Nick wanted to work on his son's problems, parent coaching is about helping individuals meet parenting challenges. He needed to work through his anxious emotions before assisting Sam. Only then was he able to shift his thinking from survival to transformational. Nick began by asking himself what type of parent he wanted to be to his son. What kind of relationship did he want with him? Looking at what we wrote, he realized he needed to change how he interacted with Sam. He had to take the focus off his need to make sure his son was safe and to nurture a more supportive relationship.

Gradually, Nick changed the way he communicated with Sam. Rather than scolding or threatening, he adopted a calmer approach. He asked questions like, "What choices do you have?" and "What have you decided to do?" Nick realized that his son was responsible for his own academic success, and Nick's role was to be supportive. He held Sam accountable by engaging him with questions, offering support, and providing encouragement to help him stay on the right path.

Instead of dictating what Sam should do, Nick inquired about any obstacles or challenges affecting Sam's progress. And when he did have advice to share, he took a moment to ask Sam if he could offer some guidance. Surprisingly, Sam often welcomed and appreciated Nick's advice when it was given in this way.

When his grades didn't improve, Sam needed to rethink whether his electrical engineering major was a good fit for him. He approached his dad and asked, "Can you help me think about what I should do?" Nick was grateful for the invitation and worked with Sam to find new pathways.

Transformational thinking will help you define who you are, create better relationships, and even manage your ADHD monkeys better. Take a moment to answer these identity questions: Who do you want to be? How do you want others to describe you? What kind of partner do you want to be? What kind of brother or sister, son or daughter? How do you want to live your life? Are you meeting your own standards? Use the table near the end of the chapter to help you determine which thoughts and behaviors are survival and which are transformational.

> Who do you want to be? How do you want others to describe you? What kind of partner do you want to be? What kind of brother or sister, son or daughter? How do you want to live your life? Are you meeting your own standards?

Knowing that we cannot always be our best transformational thinking self is essential. Hunger, fatigue, illness, and intense emotions will knock us off-kilter and place us smack-dab in survival thinking. And for those of us with ADHD and a narrow window of tolerance, it doesn't take much to drop into survival thinking. A change in our schedule (or almost any transition), not getting enough sleep, and our persistent short-term memory issues all contribute to our dependency on survival thinking. Survival thinking may feel comfortable, but we can incorporate transformational thinking into our daily lives when we practice.

The Time Machine

Survival and transformational thinking would have been so beneficial for me to know throughout my life. While others might use a time machine to defy quantum gravity for more grand purposes, I would use it to visit younger versions of myself to help her on her journey.

Just for fun: Can you spot the survival thinking in the examples in the previous chapters?

I'd start by visiting my twenty-something self. In addition to telling her about the basics of ADHD, I'd introduce the concept of transformational thinking. I'd assure her that no one feels settled in their twenties because it's a time to figure out what their life will look like and to become independent. I'd tell her there are two different versions of ourselves—one trying to impress the world and the authentic one wanting to be good for the world. "While trying to figure it out," I'd say lovingly, "decide which values you want to carry. And if you can, learn to spot the times when you see your authentic, transformational-thinking self."

It would not be easy to find time to visit my thirty-something self. She was working as a full-time professor, progressing toward her PhD, and busy trying to meet the needs of her three treasured young children. She spent the decade exhausted and depleted. Maybe I'd visit her home in those early morning moments before her mind started sprinting. "I know you are busy," I'd whisper. "I know you are doing your best. You feel the pressure to do a lot at this stage of life. You don't need to be everything to everyone. Please challenge the belief that you need to prove something to someone somewhere. Breathe and nurture the part of you that loves truth, beauty, and goodness."

I can't be sure that either of those younger selves would trust a time traveler, but I am positive that my forty-something self would. She was ready for change. I'd be direct and say, "Listen, it's time you lay down some of the tendencies that you've developed. This thing you do with holding grudges doesn't really work. It hurts you and your ability to think in a transformational way. And are you aware that you get sucked into other people's emotions? That is certainly a part of your ADHD, but could you begin to address that?" I know she would look back at me seriously and say, "Got it," then head toward the self-help section of a bookstore.

But there's no time machine, and I've learned that there's no such thing as "being done" when developing your transformational-thinking self. Each day, I have endless opportunities and challenges that can knock me over to the survival mindset. But because these opportunities exist daily, they also allow me to mature.

Be patient with yourself as you grow. Even if no one in your family practices transformational thinking, you can—and that will make a difference, if only in yourself.

While survival thinking may seem like a comfortable fallback, the good news is that we can integrate transformational thinking into our daily lives through practice. In the upcoming sections of this book, we'll delve into the different aspects of transformational thinking and how it can positively impact you and your family.

Survival and Transformational Traits

Survival	Transformational
Ego-driven	Purpose-driven
Sense of urgency	Sense of composure
Win-at-all-costs mentality	Collaborative mentality
Doesn't consider their values when reacting	Considers their values when responding
Reactive—doesn't examine their thoughts and feelings	Gains perspective—examines their thoughts and feelings before or after responding
Ruminates and perseverates	Shares opinions, thoughts, and emotions openly without infringing on others' territory
Anxious presence	Non-anxious presence
Avoids challenges	Embraces challenges
Emotionally unregulated	Emotionally regulated

Survival	Transformational
Lacks awareness of thoughts and feelings or believes they should take precedence over others' thoughts and feelings	Curious about their own thoughts and feelings, allowing space for others' perspectives
Expects others to meet their needs	Identifies and meets their own needs in healthy ways
Blames others or sees others as a problem	Takes responsibility for their own thoughts and actions
Has a conflict of wills, wanting to force their way on a situation	Problem-solves, working with others to formulate a solution
Refuses to apologize or demands an apology	Apologizes authentically when appropriate
Needs to be right	Acknowledges others' perspectives
Demands that others help them resolve their inner turmoil	Self-soothes inner turmoil
Tries to fix others or takes responsibility for others' actions	Encourages the strength they see in others, not comforting or accommodating their weakness
Acts and thinks like those they are around	Acts in ways consistent with who they are, what they believe, and what they value
Self-worth depends on approval from and pleasing others	Self-worth is not impacted by how others react to their good deed
Gets sucked into others' intense emotions (anxiety, anger, sadness)	Balances their own nervous system and has appropriate empathy

Reflection

Transforming your thinking from survival mode to a more expansive and growth-oriented mindset often involves intentional and gradual changes in your thought patterns and behaviors. Here are some strategies to help you shift toward transformational thinking:

1. *Use awareness and mindfulness.* Start by becoming aware of your thoughts and recognizing when you are in survival mode. Mindfulness practices and self-reflection can help you observe your thoughts without judgment.

2. *Identify limiting beliefs.* Explore and identify limiting beliefs or negative thought patterns contributing to survival thinking. Question the validity of these beliefs and challenge them with more positive and empowering alternatives.

3. *Practice gratitude.* Regularly express gratitude for the positive aspects of your life. This can shift your focus from scarcity to abundance and foster a more optimistic, peaceful, and transformational outlook.

4. *Embrace change and adaptability.* Accept that change is a natural part of life. Develop adaptability by seeing change as an opportunity for growth rather than a threat to your survival. Manage the scary "what if" questions that pop into your thinking. They are usually tugging you back to survival thinking.

5. *Feed yourself with positive influences.* Seek positive influences through supportive relationships, uplifting content, or environments that encourage growth. The people and media you surround yourself with can impact your mindset.

6. *Learn from mistakes.* Survival thinking views mistakes as failures. Transformational thinking sees them as opportunities to learn and improve. Analyze what went wrong, identify lessons, and use that knowledge to make better decisions in the future.

7. *Develop resilience.* Transformational thinking builds resilience by viewing challenges as temporary setbacks rather than insurmountable obstacles. Cultivate the ability to bounce back from difficulties with a positive and solution-oriented mindset.

Remember that transforming your thinking is a gradual process. Consistent effort and a commitment to positive change can lead to a shift from survival thinking to a more transformational mindset. If needed, consider seeking support from a therapist or counselor to explore these changes further.

9

SAFETY FIRST

"Are you a safe person for her?" I asked Brian.

Brian thought for a moment, looked at his wife, and replied, "Yeah, I think I am."

I then turned to Brian's wife and asked, "Are you a safe person for him?"

"Of course," Ingrid said without hesitation.

Brian sat motionless, looking as if he was holding his breath, not agreeing or disagreeing. His frozen form suggested that perhaps he wasn't feeling as safe as his wife thought.

I often ask clients about emotional safety because it is essential for an individual's mental health and the development of meaningful family relationships. Without emotional security, you can't love well or even live well. If you don't feel emotionally safe when you're with someone, you can't feel close, and you don't feel good. I ask clients if they are a safe person for their family members because in many homes affected by ADHD, people tell me they don't feel safe. Family members often don't realize their behavior may be making others feel like they are tiptoeing through a perilous obstacle, booby-trapped with Indiana Jones–type snares.

We often are unaware of how our opinions, comments, and actions affect the perception of emotional safety in a relationship. It is simpler to tell if another person is safe for us than to analyze if we are safe for them. As you read this chapter, focus on whether you are a safe person for those you love. It's tempting to let your mind wander to people in your life, especially the unsafe ones. For now, though, concentrate on how others might experience you. Use the quiz at the end of this chapter to help you find the areas where you can become even safer.

Emotional safety is not placating the ones you love, bubble-wrapping them so they never feel hurt or uncomfortable. It is something very different—and precious. It is the instinctual feeling of being accepted and embraced for who you are. Emotional safety is where you connect deeply. Author and researcher Brené Brown writes that it is "the energy that exists between people when they feel seen, heard, and valued; when they can give and receive without judgment; and when they derive sustenance and strength from the relationship."[1] Those who feel that deep connection with you reveal themselves, the parts they hide from the rest of the world. And there's potentially no better place for emotional safety than in a family.

When asked whom he feels the safest with, a client said his brother Stuart, four years younger than him. They can spend a day fishing together, barely saying a word for hours, and he feels at peace. "He's my person," he concluded. "After a day with him, I feel like I remember who I am." Although Stuart doesn't have ADHD, my client feels entirely accepted and seen by his sibling.

When someone feels emotionally safe with you, their whole body responds. Their heart rate and respiration go down and even synchronize with yours. Perspiration, a sign of stress, is reduced. The muscles in their body relax. They can even tolerate physical pain better when they're with you.

When people feel emotionally safe, their emotional system calms down, and they can better express emotions. They're likely to express more of their thoughts and feelings, both positive and negative. Their nervous system is not on alert.

Durable families have psychologically safe environments. When family members feel safe when they are together, they easily engage. It's easier to have conversations while driving to hockey practice, collaborating on chores, and solving problems. When family members feel safe, they express their ideas and fears and reveal who they are. They know that whatever they express, they are still loved. In emotionally safe families, there is a level of predictability and consistency in emotions and behaviors, including clear boundaries and expectations. When relationships are damaged, as they surely will be, repairing occurs to rebuild the bridge between the two in conflict.

In families lacking emotional security, their members feel emotionally unsafe, emotionally attacked, belittled, or simply ignored. Sarcasm is slung like fistfuls of mud at each other, and everyone anticipates the need to protect themselves. When someone doesn't feel emotionally safe, they feel emotionally threatened, which causes the same bodily reactions as feeling *physically* threatened. Their body tenses as their brain registers danger and sends the signal to fight, flee, freeze, or appease. Studies have shown that social and emotional rejection activate the same pain centers in the brain as physical injuries. Our brains don't differentiate physical and emotional pain clearly. If for some reason you are unable to find emotional safety, it is essentially like living in a state of constant physical threat.[2]

Sometimes families have created emotional safety, but there are still gaps that need filling. Kurt handed me a letter and explained why his family wanted to meet with me. He and Jill were heartbroken when their son, Lance, wrote a letter telling them that he had failed a college course. "What hurts me isn't that he failed a course; it's that he felt so ashamed and didn't know how to tell us," Kurt explained.

Because Lance's mother had helped him manage assignments in middle school and high school, he hadn't experienced failure much. "I didn't know what to do; I felt so ashamed. I wasted their money," Lance said. His parents quickly affirmed that they loved him even when the outcome wasn't what they had hoped for. That day Kurt and Jill took the opportunity to deepen their expression of emotional safety to include the message "We can talk about your failures." There was unmistakable love and respect between the parents and their child.

Although no family environment is always safe, you can be thoughtful in how you engage those you love. Consider four areas when working to become a safe person in your family: self-awareness, communication, conflict resolution, and vulnerability.

Self-Awareness

Many of my clients assume they are a safe person in their family when, in actuality, their family members tread lightly around them or hesitate to talk to them. Emmie was crushed when she realized she wasn't considered a safe person in her family. At twenty-three, she was the youngest and had begun to wonder why she wasn't as close to her siblings as she wanted. In an email, she asked her family for honest reactions and explained that she would share their emails with me so that we could learn from them. Her mother and two siblings replied with direct and valuable responses.

After reading them, Emmie fought the messages like they were accusations. "Well, they're not perfect either! They've hurt me too!"

I gently reminded her that she wanted to be good for those she loved, and that was why she came up with the idea of asking her family for feedback.

When we reviewed her family's notes, we circled her mother's words. "Honey, I love you so much, but it is difficult to be around you when you are in a bad mood. You snap at us and treat us poorly. We feel like we need to gauge your emotions before talking with you."

Emmie cried in response.

Her older brother wrote, "I know that you are a kind person, but I don't see that person often when I'm around you. . . . We all make mistakes and have bad days; I wish you would apologize when . . ."

With a similar sentiment, her older sister wrote, "I feel like if anything goes wrong, you get tense and rude. . . . Sometimes I feel hurt when I'm around you."

Emmie knew this. She warned people that she was in a bad mood and expected others to adjust their behavior, but it hadn't occurred to her to modify her own attitude or actions.

For Emmie to become who she wanted to be in her family, she needed to increase her self-awareness, especially around her emotions. She decided to concentrate on her mood management and apologize for lashing out. In the end, she responded to her family's feedback, thanking them for their honesty and sharing her goals with them:

- If I am in a negative mood, I know it's my responsibility to manage it.
- If I have a bad day and say something that hurts you, I will apologize.
- If I act in a hurtful way, I will apologize.

Her family's response was encouraging and supportive. As a result, Emmie's relationship with them strengthened. Eventually, she improved her ability to be aware of her negative emotional state and take steps to manage herself.

How about you? Are you aware of your impact on your family? Do they avoid telling you things because you will get upset? Do they feel relaxed around you, or are they on guard around you? Emmie's courageous request for feedback from her family awakened the possibility for deeper conversation and better relationships. Maybe you'll want to begin with only one person.

Select someone you know has your best interests at heart and ask questions about your emotional impact on them. Remember to listen to the responses while in a balanced state of mind.

Communication

Another area to reflect on when you are analyzing whether you have a safe presence in your family is communication. How we communicate with those we love conveys a sense of safety.

"My grandma Helen," Rick answered when I asked him to name a safe person in his family. Rick, now in his fifties, fondly recalled his time with her. "I remember talking with her while helping her with the dishes, my hands in the warm, soapy water." He smiled at the memory and added, "I always felt safe with her."

The memory of his grandma was in juxtaposition to how he was currently feeling in his family. "We are all a mess," he had told me in our previous session. "My wife has depression, my one son has anxiety and ADHD, and my other son . . . I don't even know. He's complicated. We can't get a handle on it. And then there's me, with my ADHD and all." He was tense and nervous as he talked about his family's current situation. He explained that he hadn't been helping the family environment much. Most of the time, he told me, he debated with, urged, prompted, and cajoled other family members. He wanted to be less anxious and more peaceful around them and sought ways to communicate that.

"What did your grandmother do to communicate she was safe?" I asked.

After a bit of silence, he said, "I remember when I was ten, I told her I thought I saw a UFO. She was truly interested in what I experienced. She didn't judge me or tell me that I was a stupid kid and that it was probably a weather balloon or something. Instead, she asked me what I saw and thought of it. I told her how I wrote a story about aliens. I explained my theory that they were nice travelers who were sightseers." His grandmother gave him the impression that she was fully present during their chat. "When I asked her not to tell my father about what I had seen, she assured me that she wouldn't say anything."

His grandmother listened nonjudgmentally, validated his experience, and was trustworthy. Over forty years later, he remembers how she made him feel.

"I want my family to feel like that around me," Rick said wistfully, still in the sweet memory of his grandmother. He made a list of the characteristics he could display around his family:

- Listening nonjudgmentally
- Validating their experience or emotion
- Showing compassion
- Being trustworthy (not sharing sensitive information)
- Displaying complete acceptance and respect

"The last one is particularly important for me. It's a high value of mine," Rick added. "I want my wife and kids to feel completely loved and accepted." He then began to work on becoming a safer person for his family.

How about you? Safe people communicate their safety in various ways. Still, at the heart of it, the safest people are kindhearted, offer grace, and look for goodness in others. Do others feel relaxed around you, or are they on guard? Are you communicating emotional safety to those you love? Do you ask how you can be supportive when your loved ones are experiencing difficulty? Asking those you love for feedback will help you communicate your love to them more effectively.

Conflict Resolution

Being a safe person during a disagreement is challenging. Although you may want to be safe, everything in you frequently feels the need to protect yourself, push back, blame, or argue.

Maria and Jason loved each other, but their conflicts left marks that affected their lives together. Maria was "well-defended," as her husband pointed out. When he tried to approach a topic by sharing what he was experiencing, she was quick to reframe it for him. Drawing logical conclusions to support her position, she bombarded Jason with alternative rationales. His feelings didn't matter. Although she looked poised and in control of her emotions, she had become adept at a pseudo-diplomatic style of discussing topics that kept her from honestly engaging in meaningful discussions with her spouse. Jason dug an emotional trench to protect himself in response to her artillery-style discussion. He shut down anytime conflict was on the horizon.

Though they were trying to have healthy conflict, they both tripped over safety guidelines:

- Don't argue with the other's lived experiences or feelings, even if you disagree with them.
- Do not rush to fix or solve.
- Do not give unsolicited advice.

Because Maria wanted a better relationship and hated how she and Jason never seemed to resolve their arguments, she tried to find a better way. She started developing the most essential skill—active listening. Active listening ensures people feel valued and can express what they think and feel. The apparently simple task of active listening is staying focused on the person and what they are saying, which is arduous work for those of us with ADHD.

It wasn't until I was trained as a coach that I realized how much I listened egocentrically, with the what's-in-it-for-me filter engaged. Listening to others' feelings and discussing issues without factoring myself into the equation is difficult if I don't focus my attention. And listening to someone talk about how my behavior affects them without being defensive is very challenging and nearly impossible if I am in survival thinking.

Maria became a listener who was invested in Jason's thoughts. "It's still hard to listen to him when I think he's wrong," she said with a laugh. Then, hearing herself, she added, "I mean, maybe he's not wrong just because I disagree."

When Jason expressed frustration or other painful emotions, she learned to ask how he would like to be supported. Together, they established clear boundaries around what is okay and what is not okay to say during conflict, making it safe for them both. Though the process took several months, she noticed that their relationship did improve.

Vulnerability

Being emotionally safe means that you are willing to take a risk to show your primary emotions and express them honestly, despite fears of rejection. When you're vulnerable, you can build trust with others by:

- Being transparent and expressive
- Readily admitting mistakes
- Apologizing when you're wrong
- Having difficult conversations

Vulnerability can make it safe for others to share their thoughts and feelings.

Personally, I don't care very much for vulnerability. It makes me feel like I'm in my recurring dream of showing up late to teach a class—in a towel. Don't get me wrong. I am a big fan of the queen of vulnerability, Brené Brown, and I have read many of her books, but I still get a slight menacing shiver when I take off my armor and choose vulnerability. There are times when I am around friends and acquaintances and feel like a second-rate mother/wife/business owner/coach/author. I am tempted to engage my survival thinking, put my guard up, and pretend that I am stronger and smarter than I am. Instead, I take a deep breath, feel the cold shiver, remind myself of what transformational thinking looks like—and step toward authenticity.

Don't confuse vulnerability with the ADHD characteristic of oversharing or overexplaining. Oversharing is saying something personal or inappropriate in the wrong setting or to the wrong person. Sometimes we may not realize it, and suddenly, we find ourselves offering too much information or saying the wrong thing. Who among us with ADHD hasn't had the experience of sitting on a plane and finding ourselves sharing the intimate details of our lives with a total stranger? Then we get off the plane, embarrassed, hoping never to see that person again. Vulnerability, on the other hand, is a deliberate act of self-disclosure to those we trust that allows us to build deeper and more meaningful connections with them.

Past Hurts

Can we be emotionally safe for someone when we don't feel safe ourselves? Some of us have felt the sting of being picked on by our family members, feeling that the people who matter most or those we depend on most for survival don't really see us. And for whatever reason, they can't meet our needs or address our feelings. We haven't felt safe for a while, if ever. As a result, many of us have regarded our emotions and thoughts as unacceptable, unlovable, and even contemptible.

Life is full of experiences like this, past and present. We may have also experienced this outside our family, at a previous job, or while in school in ways that have left invisible but deep-rooted scars. It's typical to respond to a lack of safety by protecting ourselves from ever feeling that kind of pain again. We avoid any risk of being attacked or shunned. Sadly, the same reactions we use to shield ourselves from more significant harm frequently make us even more isolated, clingy, or miserable. Those who feel chronically unsafe can sometimes become unsafe to others.

Although it is easier and safer to remain in our old protective patterns, the brave will try to find ways to heal their experiences to ensure those they love will feel safe around them. Learning to be safe is deciding not to continue a pattern but instead to change how others experience us.

Emotional safety is a basic human need and an essential building block for healthy relationships. In your own life, the first step to building more emotional safety is to realize that you and everyone around you *need* it more than you—or they—think. Emotional safety comes when people treat each other with care and respect. Families affected by ADHD will still include joking and playfulness, but it won't be at someone's expense. You can be a safe person in your family by loving and accepting your family members for who they are and allowing them to feel how they feel. You can be the person who makes them feel seen, heard, and understood. You can create an environment where your loved ones can be themselves without the risk of judgment.

Are you a safe person for those you love? Use this quiz to help you find the areas where you can become even safer.

Scoring: 3 = always, 2 = frequently, 1 = sometimes, 0 = never

_____ 1. If I know I'm in a negative mood, I adjust my attitude or find some space to manage my emotions.

_____ 2. If I have a bad day and say something I regret, I apologize.

_____ 3. Others feel comfortable around me.

_____ 4. If I act in a hurtful way, I apologize.

_____ 5. I am genuinely interested in others' emotional experiences. I ask how their day went and am engaged.

_____ 6. I cherish the quirky and unique parts of others that bring them joy.

_____ 7. When someone is upset or expresses an issue, I remain receptive and don't invalidate their feelings by saying, "You are always blaming me" or "You are too sensitive."

_____ 8. I listen to feedback about myself without becoming defensive or reactive.

_____ 9. I allow others to share what they feel without trying to "fix it."

_____ 10. I can have uncomfortable or tense conversations without name-calling, diagnosing, shaming, or getting out of control.

_____ 11. I don't emotionally punish others by refusing to talk to them for days.

If you scored 22–33, you believe that you are a safe person. Ask a family member what they think about your responses to this quiz to verify your results. If you scored 21 or below, select two of these statements and decide how you want to improve in those areas.

PART TWO

READY FOR
THE RODEO

10

SCORPIONS, SKUNKS, AND PESKY PECCADILLOES

I was describing the characteristics of an emotionally healthy family to a client when she put up her hand and stopped me. "You are describing a unicorn: a beautiful, fanciful idea, but unrealistic." Because some of us—myself included—weren't raised in families who modeled safety or health, we didn't develop a sense of what healthy families look like. And although we crave the love and belonging that a family offers, we may not understand what behaviors to accept and what to reject.

Generally, when a family relationship is caring, encouraging, and respectful, it is probably healthy. While no family is perfect and all will have conflict, the most emotionally healthy families provide emotional and physical safety, resolve disputes in beneficial ways, communicate respectfully, and learn to compromise and collaborate.

The first nine chapters of this book helped us focus on becoming a healthy presence for our family members. But what if our family members aren't a safe or healthy presence for us? Learning to identify problematic relationships can help us take practical actions to reduce emotional suffering or distress. We can classify behaviors before they erode our self-esteem and hinder our personal growth. There are three categories of family behaviors, and for ease of remembering, I've assigned an animal to each: scorpion, skunk, and armadillo.

Toxic Scorpions

"My wife told me that I need help for my ADHD because she can't stand it any longer," a client shared. I nodded because I know it can be challenging to live with someone with ADHD. But then he told me about an event with his wife that went beyond the challenges of having ADHD. He ended his story with a sigh. "I need help. She says that I'm lazy and that I lie."

"Lie?"

"Yes, like when I say I'll do something and then don't. She calls that lying."

"Do you think it's lying?"

He looked confused. He tried to explain but then gave up. "I'm trying to fix myself the best that I can." His voice cracked as the emotion came to his throat. "She's told me that I'm toxic and a narcissist."

"Has anyone, friends or family, expressed concern for you and this relationship?" I asked.

The question took him by surprise. "Well, I don't really talk about my marriage to many people, but my dad tells me my wife is much like my mother. They were divorced when I was in high school. She passed away when I was in my late twenties."

My question "What are the similarities?" set him back for a moment. Then the similarities spilled out. He described feeling ensnared in a series of mind games, belittling comments, and confusion about what was true.

We were quiet momentarily as what he had just said settled in.

"I want to coach you on managing your ADHD behaviors, but I wonder if you want to talk to a therapist too," I said. "Your description of your relationship causes me to think that it is important to resolve some issues. Could I help you find someone?"

This first category, the scorpion, represents toxic behavior. It is the most severe and demands serious attention. I'd like you to imagine the fat-tailed scorpion of Tunisia. This thick, translucent, yellow predatory arachnid is responsible for 90 percent of deaths from scorpion stings in North Africa. The neurotoxins in the venom can kill a person within six hours. You can't afford to be in proximity to this guy. The fat-tailed scorpion directly injects poison into its victims. Likewise, the scorpion in the family injects toxins by undermining one's well-being through strict control, emotional manipulation, and blatant disrespect.

A toxic person may need to control another person in a relationship. There is an unequal power dynamic, usually with one person dominating another in a self-serving manner. The scorpion sees your success as a threat and may always try to one-up you or put you back in your place. You may learn that your successes and interests do not matter as much as theirs do. They may even want you to spend all your free time with them, which could isolate you from friends and family and deprive you of your independence and other activities you may enjoy.

You can often recognize that someone is a scorpion by how they communicate with you and others. They may be very sarcastic and critical of you while covering it up by stating that they were "only joking," convincing you that you are too sensitive. Another trick of this toxic arachnid is to find fault with everything you do and blame you for everything negative that happens, never accepting blame themselves. When you explain your emotional needs to them, they turn it around so that you end up comforting them instead. You eventually learn that they will become angry and punish you if you share your feelings or unhappiness with them. Although they often try to orchestrate relationships to serve their own ends, they try to gain sympathy and attention by claiming victim status. Ultimately, their manipulation, lying, passive-aggressiveness, and gaslighting leave you confused and questioning your sanity.

Cruel emotional treatment, violence, and sexual abuse are characteristics of toxic disrespect. A scorpion disrespects you consistently because they don't value your personhood or boundaries since their needs are too strong and too often take precedence.

Although the fat-tailed scorpion is not a pet, some of us may consider them or have had them as roommates. Although anyone can fall victim to toxic behavior, certain types of people are more susceptible to toxic people.

There are many reasons why those of us with ADHD are vulnerable to scorpions. We may miss signs that someone is behaving problematically or forget earlier signs to see the pattern. We may forget the details of events, so the other person can convince us of their narrative, otherwise known as gaslighting. There is also the issue that if we are used to being told we're the one who made a mistake, we may be more tolerant of a partner who is happy to shift the blame. Some of us with ADHD are emotionally vulnerable to toxic people because we trust others easily, openly show admiration for others, and defend those we care about. In addition, many of us learn to develop our ability to relate to the emotions of those around us. Although those aren't negative characteristics, toxic family members see our poor boundaries, unregulated empathy (see chapter 16), and sensitive hearts as fuel for their egos.

When Tara talked about what drew her to her first husband, Kevin, she said, "He just seemed to have his act together. I liked that because I felt like my ADHD prohibited me from feeling confident." She also liked how he seemed in control of his emotions—so different from the emotional chaos she grew up with. Tara described herself as a person who wore her heart on her sleeve. She loved the rush of love she felt when she met Kevin. "Now I realize that it was a dopamine surge," she reflected.

Those of us with ADHD have difficulty regulating dopamine, the "feel-good hormone," in our brains. Although new relationships provide an incredible and addicting thrill for everyone, those with ADHD can get lost in the feeling.

Tara noticed certain patterns after marriage: "Some days, not often, he would be amazing, and I would feel amazing too. Then other times, he would just be so mean, so horrible, like he hated me. It was confusing. And it tapped into my self-loathing."

Those with ADHD frequently take their emotional cues from those close to them. Tara and Kevin's relationship exhibited the poisonous characteristics of control, manipulation, and disrespect. Like many others, Tara carried painful memories and emotions of past ADHD-related failures. Recollections of being punished for not turning in homework, missing deadlines, arriving late to work, and not cleaning her room taught her to apologize frequently for imperfections and cemented her tendency toward self-loathing.

"He preyed on my empathy and people pleasing too," Tara said. "I felt sorry for him all the time. And I'd try to help him feel better about himself."

Many of us with ADHD have learned to be people pleasers, mistakenly believing we have no value unless we do something for someone else. A scorpion is attracted to those of us who have unregulated empathy because our caring nature means that we are likely to do as much as we can to ensure that others will be happy, even when it is harmful to us.

"Looking back, I didn't understand what nontoxic relationships looked like," Tara admitted. "Toxicity looked normal to me."

If you find yourself on the receiving end of any of these behaviors, please do not try to resolve them alone. Seek safety and the help of a trusted professional. It may be that severing ties in this situation is the only way that you can resolve it.

Noxious Skunks

It is normal to experience times when you don't feel cared for, encouraged, or respected by your family members. Someone may not have given you the hoped-for response, and you feel discouraged. Or maybe you tried to share a profound thought with a family member, and they were too busy to understand what you were trying to say. Sometimes we have differing opinions in families, and the way disagreements are handled leaves us disappointed, angry, or sad. Feeling let down by family members does not necessarily mean the relationship is toxic. You may have just experienced some skunky behavior.

Skunks are small, furry animals with black-and-white stripes. Don't let their adorable appearance fool you. Their coloring is a warning sign to anyone interacting with this creature. They are known for their ability to spray a liquid with a strong, unpleasant odor from their scent glands that can last for three weeks. For those of you who don't live in North, Central, or South America, where skunks are indigenous, you may not have had the unfortunate opportunity to smell the notorious noxious fumes. Think of the smell as a mix of marijuana, burning rubber, and rotten eggs.

Noxious skunk describes harmful, unpleasant, and possibly poisonous behaviors that have a detrimental influence on you. The skunky tendencies frequently originate from a combination of egocentrism and emotional dysregulation. Unlike those in the toxic scorpions category, skunks are not intentionally trying to manipulate you. Instead, they are consumed with their own self-centered thoughts at that moment.

People who display noxious behavior aren't thinking beyond their feelings. They may refuse to compromise, not show concern for your feelings, or not apologize for their behavior. Their egocentricity stinks up the room as they blame others, throw emotional fits, and make passive-aggressive comments.

When Jayden vigorously scolds her husband for dropping a light bulb, she isn't thinking about his thoughts or feelings. She is focused on her annoyance at the mess of the broken light bulb. She wants to make sure, in her own rationalization, that he knows he was careless. She sprays a foul odor like a skunk, leaving her husband feeling ashamed, embarrassed, or angry.

Does this behavior sound familiar? Noxious behavior happens when we are stuck in survival thinking (chapter 8), have an unbalanced nervous system (chapters 6 and 7), and make all sorts of emotional mistakes (chapter 5). The truth is that unless we work at it, we can be skunky too.

Sometimes adults with ADHD react with big emotions when things don't go according to expectations. Even minor irritations and disruptions can cause them to overreact with an outburst or meltdown, making it hard to complete tasks and maintain relationships.

Leah, reflecting on the noxious fumes her family created when she was a child, said, "We had a good family and all, but whenever my dad got angry, he'd start blaming anyone and getting snappy. We'd make ourselves scarce when that happened." She had grown up in a home where tempers frequently flared, accusations were launched, and insults were hurled. Although her parents had passed away, the family patterns persisted.

Leah was talking about spending the upcoming holiday with her brother and sister. I knew from previous sessions that ADHD ran in her family. Her siblings had what sounded like undiagnosed ADHD, and neither had good emotional management. Her siblings weren't aware of their noxious behavior and considered the blowups part of a usual holiday. In our coaching session, we talked about sustaining Leah's emotional regulation during the festivities. "I think I've been working on this for so long that I'll be fine," she said.

The following week she started the session by saying, "I underestimated how noxious the fumes still are." She described a series of small but intense events that drained her. Although she rebalanced her nervous system and remained in transformational thinking, she still was overcome with the stink of emotional volatility. "It just stank—and it was exhausting," she said. "So I made an excuse to get away from that smell. I took the kids to the park—a lot." Still, Leah considered her experience positive. "We had some good times. And when the skunks sprayed, I managed myself instead of trying to manage the skunk." She avoided the stink and did not try to pet the skunk.

Because a skunky family member is acting in survival mode, it isn't likely that you will be able to reason with them. Remember, those in survival thinking aren't willing to problem-solve.

But what do you actually do when a skunk is around? First, manage yourself, and don't get caught in the stink. Think about your nervous system. Are you in your window of tolerance? If not, use the techniques in chapter 7 to regain your composure. Then check your thinking. Are you feeling fed up because you are trying to help the other person see reality, explain how you think, defend your actions, and get them to calm down? You may have slipped into survival thinking. You don't have to explain, justify, or defend yourself or deal with a misfired accusation. Focus on regaining your transformational thinking. If you can remain calm, listen to what the person is trying to communicate. This is a great time to practice self-differentiation. Separate your own intellectual and emotional functioning from that of your family members. Listening doesn't mean that you are agreeing or that you are an emotional punching bag.

If you cannot achieve balance in your nervous system and in your thinking, or if you are still feeling uncomfortable, leave the situation, letting the other person know you will come back after you both are calm. Later, if possible, when both of you are calm, discuss not only the topic itself but also how the topic was discussed. If it is an option, family counseling is a great way to identify skunky behaviors and establish better patterns.

Peccadilloes and Armadillos

No matter how hard I've tried to get my clients to think otherwise, when they hear the word *peccadillo*, they think of an armadillo, the odd-looking animal covered in bony plates. In fact, their insistence on picturing an armadillo led me to name the other categories after animals. Although Spanish in origin, *peccadillo* is a word frequently used in England that means a very minor or slight sin or offense. It is, as a Brit might say, "a trifling fault."

Many of my clients are amused with the rhyming of the two words. "When I hear you say *peccadillo*," one client explained, "I imagine two armadillo roommates conversing. One complains about the other not doing the dishes. The other shrugs and says, 'It's only a little problem.'"

Some clients already know the word because it was part of Moira Rose's eccentric lexicon in *Schitt's Creek*. Since downsizing from an extravagantly wealthy life to living in a small hotel room, she and her husband, Johnny, noticed each other's annoying habits:

Moira: In a room this tiny, we've just got to ignore the little irritants of the other, or you'd go insane!

Johnny: Little irritants? What, uh, what little irritants? I have little irritants?

Moira: Yes, we all do. Peccadilloes, cloying habits.

Johnny: Like what, for instance?

Moira: All right, John. I—I drink a little too much tea sometimes.

Johnny: And that's it for you? You, uh, you drink tea?

Moira: Well, it calms me, so I suppose you would say that's because I'm inclined to get nervous or insecure.

Johnny: No, I would say you're sometimes a little defensive and, uh, perhaps a tad paranoid.

Moira: That would only be after you've taken that condescending father tone with me.[1]

Moira and Johnny continue to squabble about the unimportant and annoying habits of the other for the rest of the scene.

Peccadilloes are the irritating things our family members do, like leaving cupboard doors open, interrupting us when we are talking, running late every morning, depositing their shoes and other articles of clothing throughout the house, and making smacking noises while eating. I'm sure you can name a few of your family members' annoying traits now.

Peccadilloes cause significant problems in families because they get blown out of proportion. Since we can't see our family members' inner thoughts, we judge their actions and assume they are doing them due to some character trait or moral failure—they are lazy or are trying to aggravate us. We need to be careful of making a fundamental attribution error, a well-known phenomenon, when we explain someone's behavior based on internal factors, such as personality, character traits, or a moral failing. On the other hand, we blame our own behavior on external factors. For example, I might say my mom didn't return my call because she's passive-aggressive, but I didn't return my mom's call because I've been so busy. In other words, we tend to cut ourselves a break and blame circumstances while holding others entirely accountable for their actions.

Fundamental attribution errors tend to happen when we are negatively affected by someone's behavior. We imagine what the other person was thinking or what negative trait could lead them to their decision, and we assume negative characteristics or intentions without questioning our accuracy. We forget to consider if their action could have resulted from an external influence, a difference in preferences, an issue of priorities, or unclear communication. Not only could our judgment be wrong, but when we commit a fundamental attribution error, we are also elevating a minor infraction to a higher level.

Peccadilloes cause many issues in families affected by ADHD for two reasons: (1) Those of us with ADHD can have many bothersome habits ourselves, and (2) We often feel strongly about other people's irksome behaviors. Perhaps your ADHD quirk of clicking your pen as you study annoys your brother, and you expect him to overlook it because you're trying to focus. When he snaps his gum, however, you completely lose your composure and accuse him of deliberately trying to irritate you.

Perceiving Self **Perceiving Others**

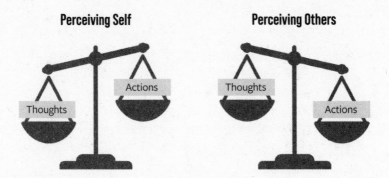

Family members exhaust themselves bickering about minor offenses like this. If you are going to survive in your ADHD family, you will need to be able to discern the peccadilloes that your family members exhibit from noxious and toxic traits. The next chapter discusses your options when challenged with someone's peccadilloes.

Unicorns

Healthy families affected by ADHD might seem rare, like finding unicorns, but they exist. What sets them apart are excellent and caring relationships, good communication, and a supportive and respectful atmosphere. These families prioritize the well-being of their emotional bonds. They know that they aren't perfect and that they still face challenges, but conflicts are fewer, are less intense, and get resolved quicker and better. There are safe spaces in these families where everyone can openly express themselves, share their feelings, and seek help when needed. These families value showing emotions. Members are encouraged to feel their emotions thoroughly and are helped in finding healthy ways to deal with them.

11

PECCADILLOES AND PREFERENCES

Let me tell you about my husband's annoying habit. After diligently washing his hands at the kitchen sink, he vigorously shakes off the excess water with reckless abandon, creating an impromptu aquatic display. I've stayed drier at Disney's Splash Mountain. It's as if his hands have taken on a mission to baptize every nearby object. My annoyance isn't about his commitment to hygiene, which is commendable, but instead about the inadvertent aftermath of his actions—the droplets of water splatter indiscriminately, leaving moisture on surrounding surfaces. Although this behavior isn't new, it remains irksome after many years of marriage. It's a peccadillo.

Chapter 10 introduced the idea of peccadilloes, those minor missteps of our family members that drive us bananas. Sometimes that predictable handwashing peccadillo peeves me more than usual, especially when I am tired, hungry, or in survival thinking. This tiny flaw in an otherwise delightful life partner can manage to unravel my threads of patience. Although I recognize the insignificance of his transgression, the irritation often persists, and I sigh as I look at the splattered kitchen window. Sometimes I tuck it away and wait for the next peccadillo and then the next, and eventually snap and let him know about all his misdemeanors at once. But peccadilloes don't need to lead to struggles, scuffles, or skirmishes.

Numerous familial disputes emerge due to clashes between preferences and peccadilloes. Lynn prefers that all her children's bedrooms be tidy: beds made, toys put away, and laundry in the hamper. She and her twelve-year-old daughter, Ainsley, argue about her bedroom's upkeep on a regular basis. In addition to dirty clothing mixed with clean clothing strewn across the floor, boxes of treasures lay open, their contents scattered across the floor. One of Ainsley's peccadilloes is collecting ordinary stuff in shoeboxes, like Starburst candy wrappers, rocks she found while playing outside, and unsharpened colorful pencils. Both Lynn and Ainsley are tired of the daily arguments.

Skirmishes between preferences and peccadilloes can harm relationships by increasing negative emotions, creating a hostile atmosphere, and hindering effective communication. Frequent arguments about a preference often lead to resentment, a sense of being unheard, and a weakened emotional connection between individuals.

When I first met Lynn, she told me, "As a parent, I have a right to ask Ainsley to do those things." Although she was correct, I hoped she would eventually reframe her feelings as a preference for a tidy room that clashed with Ainsley's many peccadilloes. Unfortunately, many parents believe that their child's behavior needs to be the first to change. Most times, it is the parents' reaction to the behavior that needs to change first.

So, what do we do when we have a peccadillo versus preference clash? The more enlightened among us will suggest that we view our preference/peccadillo conflict as an opportunity to learn, grow, and deepen our relationships rather than as a catalyst for discontent. And yes, that is the best way to go about managing this conflict. The problem is that we feel self-righteous about our preference and elevate our desire to an ethical level, believing that we are promoting a morally correct behavior. After all, what self-respecting person wouldn't reach for a kitchen towel instead of shaking excess water with reckless abandon?

When I use the hand-spritzing example in a workshop, people come to my defense, saying, "Well, you are right, it makes a mess. He should change," or, "If he really loved you, he'd change." Although their validation of my penchant for a dry kitchen briefly makes me feel smug, I need to remember that I have a preference and my husband has a peccadillo. In order to address his peccadillo, I need to be in a transformational mindset (chapter 8). If I'm in a survival mindset, I'm stuck in an egocentric perspective and believe that my preferences are the only ones that matter. So, before trying to address anyone's peccadillo, I need to do my homework first:

- Ensure that I manage my emotions about the peccadillo.
- Balance my nervous system.
- Think in a transformational mindset.

If you demand that another person change a peccadillo, you probably haven't done your homework yet. When you are disturbed by someone's peccadilloes, you essentially have three options: let it go, set guidelines for yourself, or problem-solve.

Option 1: Let it go. Pretend that you are Elsa from Disney's computer-animated adventure *Frozen.* Her self-empowering anthem, "Let It Go," can remind you to accept another person's peccadilloes. Instead of trying to correct my husband's frenzied handwashing, I let it go. And sometimes I need to let it go again. It is an irritating habit that doesn't harm anything. I remind myself of the song as I wipe the kitchen window without holding a grudge or mumbling under my breath. I also remember that I have annoying foibles and I irritate others with my peccadilloes.

Option 2: Set guidelines for yourself. Boundaries are rules we set for ourselves based on our values and priorities. They are the physical, emotional, and mental limits we establish for our mental well-being. Greta, a mother of three, grew tired of playing hide-and-seek with her family's dirty laundry. She'd look in sports equipment bags for dirty uniforms, under beds for underwear, and in the sofa cushions for socks. As you can imagine, this family peccadillo affected her time. And to add to the problem, her family blamed her when something wasn't magically cleaned and replaced in their closets or dressers. "Where are my jeans?" someone would bellow from across the house. She had become the keeper of the family's wardrobe.

Instead of assuming that her family members were passive-aggressive, disrespectful, or stupid, Greta made a guideline for herself. She calmly told her family of her boundary. "I'm going to do the laundry that finds its way to the laundry baskets next to the washer. If it's in there, it'll get washed."

Boundaries are not mandates or demands for other people to follow. Psychologist and ADHD expert Ari Tuckman says that when a person makes boundaries, they essentially say, "I'm not telling you what to do; I'm telling you what I will do."[1]

Greta's matter-of-fact tone demonstrated that she didn't want to take revenge on her family or shame them into compliance. She needed this boundary to help her manage her time more effectively. Greta needed to spend less time hunting for clothing, so she made a rule for herself and not for others. She chose not to explain her boundary or negotiate her new laundry terms because if she had, her children would negotiate the finer details of her boundary, asking questions like, "What if it's in the laundry room but not in the basket?"

There was an adjustment period where uniforms weren't ready for game day, and frustrations arose in the home. Greta stayed calm, allowing her family to accept her choice or disagree with it. Either way, she was not responsible for their responses. The family eventually found a way to deposit their laundry in the baskets.

Option 3: Problem-solve. Because nothing else seemed to work, Lynn chose this option and decided to problem-solve with her daughter about her disorganized bedroom. She decided to take Ainsley out for ice cream because conversations like this are often most productive when everyone is calm. As they sat at the picnic table with their tasty treats, Lynn began. "I have a problem when your room is not cleaned up." She owned the problem because Ainsley didn't have a problem with her disorderly room. Stating the problem and owning it is the first step. "And although it is a preference, I also want to teach you how to do certain things," Lynn continued. "I don't like when we fight. And I don't think you like it when we fight about your room either. Are you willing to work with me?"

This option only works if both parties are agreeable. And fortunately, Ainsley wanted to work with her mom.

Lynn later reflected on her mindset. "If I hadn't been in transformational thinking, I would have been tempted to blame her for being messy, lazy, or not caring what I think." Instead, she presented Ainsley with the opportunity for them to work together.

They spent some time that day identifying problem areas, brainstorming, and discussing possible solutions. "Some of the solutions Ainsley proposed were too extreme. For example, she proposed that I remove everything from her bedroom except her bed," Lynn said. "But when I observed that she liked spending time in her room coloring and reading, Ainsley agreed that it was too drastic, so we took that option off the table."

They decided to simplify the task of making her bed. Instead of pulling up sheets, blankets, and bedspread and arranging multiple pillows and stuffed animals, Lynn bought a duvet cover for Ainsley's quilt. When Ainsley wakes up, she pulls up the duvet cover and places one pillow at the top of the bed. Voilà! Two easy steps helped Ainsley accomplish the task. They both felt great about the solution. Through problem-solving, Lynn and her daughter collaborated and converted what used to cause strife in their home into a growth opportunity for both. Lynn accepted her daughter's peccadilloes while still imparting essential domestic habits.

"I can't believe how this has changed our relationship," she said. Their previous win-lose disputes diminished, and their connection deepened as they solved problems. Lynn told me a year later, "At the time, I couldn't see that I was correcting her so much that I was becoming hypercritical and she felt judged. And the more frustrated I was, the more disconnected we became."

The problem-solving approach has helped them solve many issues unrelated to chores. Just recently, Ainsley approached Lynn with a school concern, saying, "This is a problem for me. Can we work together to figure this out?" Problem-solving not only addressed the peccadillo but also helped Ainsley develop important life skills.

There is a fourth option: Stick to your preferences like they came down from Mount Sinai as a moral imperative. Remind your family how they are failing to meet your expectations. Insist that you are correct and that they are wrong, adding shame and condemnation whenever useful. It won't nurture relationships, but at least you'll rest well knowing that you're right.

All your family members have irritating quirks. I'm sure you can name them. Your children leave a trail of wrappers, socks, and toys, marking where they have been. Your uncle picks at his teeth after dinner. Your mother is always over half an hour late. We need to recognize minor imperfections in others as peccadilloes and accept that our preferences differ. When we do that, we can approach disagreements with empathy and a willingness to compromise.

12

GOING FOR A SWIM

Aletta arrived home after attending Wyatt's parent-teacher conferences at his middle school. The teacher's words rang in her head. "I just can't seem to keep his attention. He's falling behind. He may need to repeat a grade."

Pulling into the driveway, Aletta sighed as she reviewed the conversation again. "He has inattentive ADHD," she'd reminded the teacher. But her voice was quieter than usual and unsure as she said, "He has a 504 plan that provides accommodations." The teacher seemed unaware of what Aletta was saying and continued outlining her concerns. Aletta was tired, frustrated, and sad.

Now, as she walked into her kitchen carrying the groceries she'd picked up on the way home, her foot knocked against something. There in the middle of the hallway was Wyatt's backpack.

"Wyatt!" Aletta shouted. How many times had she told him to place his backpack in the lockers by the back door? Instantly her fatigue and frustration boiled into anger. All her attempts to organize and manage him weren't working. "Wyatt!" she yelled again.

Her high school daughter came into the kitchen and asked when dinner was going to be ready. Aletta snapped at her, "As soon as

I can make it!" Her daughter slunk away, mumbling that she was just asking a question and hated living there.

"Wyatt!" Aletta screeched again.

Wyatt appeared at the foot of the stairs, looking into the kitchen. "What?"

"What do you mean, 'What?'" Aletta retorted.

A brief skirmish ensued about responsibility and respect. It ended with Wyatt fighting back tears and going to his room. Aletta's negative mood spread like a contagion through the house. And by dinnertime, the five of them—Wyatt, Aletta, her daughter, her stepson, and her husband—sat eating dinner in awkward, sulking silence.

Emotions are contagious, and negative emotions are even more transmissible. When our family members are feeling upset or down, we are likely to join them in their negative emotions. Aletta had entered the house worried and feeling down, and her feelings grew in intensity and spread to her family. Because scenarios like this happen in families everywhere, and ADHD exacerbates them, my colleague Cam Gott and I developed a metaphor to help our clients understand their emotional responses and how to contend with big emotions in families.

Imagine a pool where all the intense versions of our emotions reside—fear, anger, joy, sadness, disgust, and surprise. As we go through our day, we interact with the pool. The closer we get to it, the more intensely we feel. And when we feel the strength of a particular emotion, we often enter the pool. That's okay—the goal isn't to avoid it altogether. Instead, we want to develop the ability to identify and manage our overwhelming emotions effectively when we do enter the pool, like skilled swimmers who confidently navigate through water.

Though everyone possesses their own reservoir of emotions, research reminds us that those with ADHD can become significantly more frustrated, lose their tempers more frequently, and are generally more excitable than non-ADHD individuals. It's like we don't have a lifeguard or a protective fence to stop us, so we enter our pool more easily.

We often find ourselves entering the pool when our amygdala signals an important emotional issue. Unfortunately, this part of the emotional brain has gotten a bad reputation as the brain's trouble-maker due to its association with fear, anxiety, and aggression (the fight-or-flight response). When someone experiences road rage and throws a smoothie into another car's window after a close call, many people refer to this aggressive behavior as an "amygdala hijack." The term was coined in 1995 by author Daniel Goleman to describe the sudden and irrational shift to a strong negative emotion.

The amygdala, however, does more than just signal when something has gone awry. It also signals when something is worth pursuing because it supports our needs. For instance, after we eat a delicious meal, the amygdala contributes to our feelings of enjoyment and happiness, leading us to seek that pleasure again. Moreover, recent research reveals that the amygdala is even more complicated than merely being responsible for securing pleasure and avoiding pain. It plays a role in various other areas, including social communication and understanding, which involve interpreting someone's intentions from their words or actions; emotions that relate to parenting and caregiving; and emotions that we connect to memories. The amygdala helps us detect and respond to any type of event that is important to us, like our need for physical safety, positive social relationships, or achievement. We enter the pool when our amygdala senses pressures and stressors of modern life, work, and relationships.

Although you can't directly control your feelings, you can adjust their intensity and messaging.

The problem with the term *amygdala hijack* is that it implies you are seized by your emotions and have little control over your situation. Although you can't directly control your feelings, you can adjust their intensity and messaging. The pool metaphor reframes your powerful emotional responses to help you identify sources of big emotions, tune in to your proximity to the pool, consider ways to interact with it, and respond in better ways when you are in it. When you use the pool metaphor in your life, you are taking actions that alter the intensity of an emotional experience. It doesn't mean suppressing or avoiding emotions. Instead, it means taking action to influence which emotions you have and how you express them.

Know Your Proximity to the Pool

As adults, we are expected to manage our emotions in ways that are socially acceptable and help us navigate our lives. When our emotions get the better of us, we end up in the pool.

Discouraged by Wyatt's teacher's comments, Aletta wandered near the edge of her pool. Stumbling over Wyatt's backpack made her lose her metaphorical emotional balance and fall into the pool. When we debriefed the backpack episode, Aletta admitted, "The safety and success of my children is a slick spot for me. I fall into the pool easily when it comes to them." Parenthood for many people brings about a heightened emotional vulnerability. "I find myself more sensitive and emotionally responsive," Aletta continued, "because I love them so much." Knowing this about herself helped Aletta learn about the idiosyncrasies of her pool immersions. In hindsight, she wished she'd taken a moment to think about the pool as she pulled into the driveway. "I think I may have been able to see how close I was to it. I may have been able to prevent myself from falling in and splashing my whole family."

Practicing pool awareness means sensing and observing where you are in relation to the pool. When you begin to feel emotion increase, imagine where you are in relationship to the pool: Are you walking toward it? Are your toes curled over the edge? Are you aware of the slippery places on the deck that could cause you to fall into it? If you are extremely close, how can you enter the pool safely without harming yourself or your relationships?

Have a Plan for When You Enter the Pool

We enter the pool in many different ways and with many different emotions. Some are surprised that they are in the pool. Befuddled by a mundane activity, they rant, "That stupid thing!" They leap into the water while trying to fix their printer, find their wallet, or remember a password. In these cases, like many ADHD people, they find themselves in the pool because of an intense emotional reaction that's out of proportion to the circumstance. Sometimes they may find themselves unexpectedly swimming because of suppressed emotions that suddenly become prominent. "My skin got clammy, and I felt like I was going to cry," a client explained after she drove past the office where she was fired three months before. Her emotions about the incident surfaced suddenly. "I was fine just a few minutes earlier, and then I found myself unexpectedly in the pool."

Other clients quietly slip into the pool and sink to the bottom, holding their breath. They are angry, sad, or ashamed about something but keep it all inside. I have a few clients who go for self-righteous swims, highly irritated with their family member's

For Parents

Young children can use the pool metaphor if you teach it to them. Some families have used LEGO people and a blue piece of paper to demonstrate the pool. Others find a big blue blanket to represent the pool, and they act out different situations.

Parents can also help their children develop plans for when they fall into the pool by identifying coping strategies to help them recover from the fall. Ginger and her seven-year-old daughter, Charlotte, brainstormed options for getting out of the pool when Charlotte had a meltdown. Drawing, putting on headphones, sitting in her play tent in her room, behavior and smugly knowing they are right. One client gets so happy when she knows she will spend time with her friends that she does what she calls a "joy jump." She tells me, "I just love meeting up with them and I know I'll have a blast, so I leap into my pool." Her friends have given her feedback that she shows up at events "too wound up."

How do you tend to enter the pool? What types of events or feelings cause you to take a dip? Are you mostly a surprised swimmer? Do you hold in your emotions and sink to the bottom of the pool? Perhaps you take a self-righteous swim. Or maybe you're a joy jumper. Learn about your patterns and how you tend to get wet. Can you find ways to experience the big emotions while keeping yourself safe and not splashing others?

No matter how you landed in the pool, it is your task to develop a way to get out of it. Because rational thought tends to diminish as you flail around in the pool, you need to think of what you want to do ahead of time, before you are submerged, so that you can safely swim to the side. Once you know you are in the pool, pause and take a deep, slow breath. Wait until your breathing is slow and regular. Pay attention to how you are feeling, including

playing with putty, and getting a long hug from a parent were some of the strategies they discussed. Then the clever mother bought several rubber duckies, wrote a word or phrase representing each strategy on the bottom of each duck, and placed them in a basket. When Charlotte is close to or in the pool, she chooses a rubber duck strategy. So when she experiences an overwhelming emotion, she has a plan to calm herself. Interestingly, she can identify when it is beneficial to use different strategies. "I choose drawing when I'm not in the pool yet, but when I'm in there, I want a hug."

Your child's coping skills—knowing what to do when they are near or in the pool—are some of the most important life skills they can develop.

whether you are hungry or tired. These factors can exacerbate your emotions and cause you to interpret them more strongly. If you can address the underlying issue (e.g., hunger, exhaustion), you can change your emotional response.

Decide if you are in hypoarousal or hyperarousal. Ask yourself, "What flotation device can help me right now?" In other words, what tools or strategies can you use to help you stay afloat, find the pool's edge, and climb out? (Look at the methods discussed in chapter 7.) It is important to determine which strategies are most useful and which ones to avoid before you are in the pool. Reassure yourself, "This is uncomfortable, but I know how to get out."

Finding your way out of the pool looks different for everyone. Some want to swim to the side as soon as possible. For others, that option doesn't seem available immediately. Oliver explains, "I get so overwhelmed by intense emotions, I just need to float there for a second. I grab ahold of a pool noodle and tread water." Instead of rushing to the side, he relaxes and experiences the big feeling. "I know that the sadness will pass." He listens to music as he calms himself. Then, after a bit, he swims to the side of the pool and climbs out.

Although it takes work, you can eventually learn to decrease the frequency of your plunges, the force at which you jump into the pool, and how long you stay in it. Aletta learned to visualize her pool and manage her emotions better. You, too, can imagine the pool and where you are in relationship to it. Understanding how you get into the pool, what you do while you are in it, and how you get out of it can help you learn about your emotional habits.

Because families often experience difficulties in regulating their individual and collective emotions, they need some pool rules to guide them. The next chapter explores some pool rules that you can use.

13

POOL RULES

Emotions are often the foundation of family memories because memories are not just facts encoded in our brains; they are covered with the emotions we felt when the facts occurred. "Remember when . . ." one family member starts, recalling a miserable camping trip when it rained the entire time and two of them had food poisoning. Stories like this are often passed around at family events now that the difficult moments have softened over time. Some will add details regarding how they felt or thought. "I was miserable. I hated everything and everyone. I wanted that weekend to end." Shared emotions within a family can be like invisible threads connecting us to each other, and they are often the foundation of family memories. Laughing together during a board game or crying together at a funeral increases the strands that connect us and deepens our knowledge of each other.

Shared emotions can also become a problem. In terms of the pool metaphor, one person is in the pool, and then others jump in and frolic. It might be either positive or negative shared emotions that cause their neurodiverse brains to connect, expanding and intensifying emotional energy as they splash around. Very often, a person who doesn't have ADHD watches the energy surge, worrying that someone will get hurt. And that does tend to happen. Eventually, things escalate to the point of something getting broken, feelings getting hurt, or someone's negative emotions detonating.

Sometimes when only one family member jumps into the pool, it leaves others feeling confused and uncomfortable. Many years ago, I bought a 1940s-style American Girl doll for my mother-in-law for Christmas. I knew that she would love playing dolls with my girls. I also knew she had always wanted a beautiful doll and her practical-minded farming family never got around to it when she was a child. When she opened the package, she gasped and began to sob. She plunged into the pool.

My young daughters' eyes narrowed on me. They asked, "Why did you make Grandma cry?" and "How quickly can you fix it?" I explained the concept of happy tears, but my girls remained dubious. Their grandmother's intense emotional response bothered them because they didn't understand it. They were learning that it's okay if we don't understand a family member's emotions. We need to provide space for individuals to have unique and separate emotions. That is why everyone is responsible for their own pool experience.

Some people appear impervious to their family member's pool experience. They seem insensitive to or unaware of the fact that someone else besides them may be in the pool. Most of the time, it's because they are overwhelmed, trying to figure out how to keep from drowning. For those with ADHD, their apparent pool egocentrism is usually due to the poor messaging to their cerebral cortex, not to their lack of care for those they love. They are so consumed by what they are experiencing that they forget others are having a response too. Learning about the pool can help those family members increase their awareness.

It's more captivating and less challenging to observe the emotional states of others, such as Aletta focusing on her daughter's bad attitude and her son's refusal to take responsibility for his possessions. This can be a pleasant distraction, allowing you to avoid dealing with your own emotional discomfort. That's why the first part of this book aims to assist you in focusing on your own emotions, beliefs, and behaviors. In terms of the pool, everyone is responsible for getting themselves out once they enter it. These specific pool rules will help establish some safeguards:

1. Acknowledge the existence of your emotional pool and know your proximity to it.
2. If you fall into the pool, it is your responsibility to find a way out.
3. Have a plan for when you do fall into the pool.
4. No pushing, shoving, or dangerous horseplay.
5. No pulling another person into your pool.
6. No competitive breath holding.
7. No cannonballs.
8. No diving.

The first three rules establish the importance of who owns the problem, which was addressed in chapter 11. Rules 4 through 8 are established to create a secure environment, prevent accidents, and promote respectful behavior among pool users. Families who decide to work on their emotions together use these rules to learn how to work with one another. If, however, you are in a family whose members have toxic or noxious tendencies and they are unwilling to grow with you, you can still apply these rules to yourself.

No Pushing, Shoving, or Dangerous Horseplay

Joking around within a family can create a strong sense of togetherness and strengthen the bond between family members. It's like a breath of fresh air that relieves stress, tension, and frustration that may arise from daily mishaps, like locking keys in a car, misplacing a jacket, or dealing with yet another broken handheld electronic device. Very often, those with ADHD have a sense of humor that seems to magically help family members find the silver lining in difficult situations, fostering a positive outlook and offering a lighter perspective when facing challenges. Funny storytelling, wordplay, and silliness can even serve as a form of play, which is especially beneficial for individuals with ADHD.

Many times, though, playful banter unintentionally turns harsh. Because it's all in the name of fun, we don't stop to think about context, the sensitivity of the individuals involved, or the family's norms. No one should feel hurt, excluded, or offended, and most importantly, no one should end up accidentally falling into the pool because of dangerous horseplay. Jokes that intend to belittle, humiliate, or demean someone are no longer lighthearted humor. Ultimately, empathy, respect, and sensitivity should guide us when we engage in humor in order to avoid causing harm to others.

Sometimes family members intentionally push one another into the pool. A child taunts, "I'm not touching you," as he moves his hands a few inches from his younger sibling's face, attempting to nudge his sibling into an emotional fit. Although siblings are masters at pushing their brothers and sisters into the pool, we all have engaged in that behavior. I frequently see the glimmer in a person's eye when they want to push someone into the pool, hoping for their own boost of dopamine.

No Pulling Another Person into Your Pool

One day when I was talking with a family about the pool metaphor, I asked twelve-year-old Benita, "What happens when you fall into the pool?"

Without missing a beat, the middle child replied, "I splash around screaming, and then I try to pull people into my pool." The rest of her family agreed.

She's not the only one who wants company in the pool. Many adults try to provoke a similar emotional response in others while in the pool. Sometimes this is a conscious choice of wanting others to feel the same misery they are, like Benita knocking down her brother's blocks and causing him to cry because she's mad about being unable to go to a neighbor's house. Other times it is an unconscious choice, like Aletta being unaware she was in the pool and tugging her husband and children in for a swim.

The best way to avoid pulling at others while in the pool is to be honest with them and yourself. If they know the metaphor, you can say, "I'm in the pool. I need a moment to swim to the side." If you can't communicate that, place yourself in time-out using one of your calming strategies or techniques from chapter 7.

No Competitive Breath Holding

I remember swimming with my friends as a child and a challenge would be issued: "Who can hold their breath the longest?" While this challenge may seem enjoyable or harmless in shallow water, it poses significant risks. It can lead to sudden fainting and drowning incidents that might go unnoticed until too late.[1]

Holding your breath is indirectly expressing negative feelings, resistance, or hostility rather than sharing openly and assertively, and it can be dangerous to yourself and your family. Passive-aggressive behavior is often driven by underlying feelings of anger, resentment, fear, or powerlessness. It shows up in various ways: ignoring or refusing to engage in communication, eye-rolling, sighing, or giving the cold shoulder as a means of expressing anger, frustration, or disapproval.

Sherwin tends to vault into the pool and hold his breath. "Sometimes, when I was a kid, I deliberately delayed doing something my dad asked me to do because I was so annoyed with him. I still do that with my wife." Sherwin habitually expresses his negative emotions or grievances indirectly through hints, insinuations, or nonverbal cues rather than openly addressing the issue.

Competitive breath holding doesn't address issues, and it hurts relationships. If you tend to sink to the bottom of your pool and hold your breath, identify the underlying emotions that caused you to fall into the pool in the first place. Are you feeling angry, resentful, or fearful? Are you relying on passive-aggressive tactics to manipulate or control the situation? Understanding and acknowledging these emotions can help you address them more directly and constructively. After you swim to the edge of the pool, you can be ready to express your emotions honestly and openly. Express your needs, concerns, and feelings directly, clearly, and respectfully. Use "I" statements to express your thoughts and emotions without blaming or criticizing others.

In toxic scorpion families or even in some noxious skunk families, you may not be able to express yourself without threats of retaliation or emotional blackmail. For you, the pool works only on an individual level as far as being aware of your proximity to it and getting yourself out.

No Cannonballs

Some of us may decide to enter our pool directly. Those who cannonball will hug their knees and attempt to enter the water with their body shaped as much like a sphere as possible. Their goal is to create a large splash to get attention and possibly to soak others.

On a recent family vacation, nineteen-year-old Corbin did a cannonball into his emotional pool. "I had been trying so hard to remain calm, but I just lost it. I unloaded on everyone. They were all on my nerves." His emotions splashed on those around him, and his actions put a damper on activities for part of the day. Fortunately, his parents knew the pool metaphor and didn't join him in the pool.

"We removed ourselves from the edge of his pool and gave him space to climb out," his dad explained. His parents took the other two children on a planned outing while Corbin stayed at the hotel. "We were bummed that it happened, but we just continued with our plans. Corbin knows it wasn't a punishment, but he needed to find a way out of the pool." By the time his family returned, Corbin had realized he wasn't getting enough sleep and apologized for his meltdown.

A client and frequent cannonballer remarked, "Sometimes I love the exaggerated emotion." He loved the emotional release after he created a spectacular spray in every direction around him. "Splat!"—he smacked his palms together—"I just let all the emotion out." Then, with a more serious tone, he added, "But that's hard on my wife." He hadn't realized that when he shouted at referees at a football game, yelled at other drivers in Atlanta traffic, or argued politics with family that he was essentially cannonballing into the pool. His wife explained that it was exhausting for her and affected their relationship. "It had nothing to do with her," he said. "I was upset about work or something around the house. I had no idea that I was splashing her too."

Those who cannonball into their pool need to understand that it affects others.

No Diving

It is difficult to see those we love in their emotional pool. We want to dive in and help them. Anyone who has taken water safety knows that one should never attempt a direct rescue of a conscious drowning person without proper training. In a panic, someone drowning will claw and climb, drowning many would-be rescuers. Instead, rescuers are advised to reach for or throw a flotation device to someone in trouble.

Thinking metaphorically, have you ever dived into a pool to help someone flailing? It gets ugly as they verbally lash out at

Ready for the Rodeo

For Parents

Debriefing pool events can help you discuss meltdowns and other mishaps. Wait until the child is out of their pool, then ask, "Are you ready to debrief what happened?" Don't ask to debrief if the child hasn't fully recovered yet. If their answer is no, respect it and allow them to remain in the calming-down place with the understanding that they can't move to another activity until this event has been discussed. Teaching that you will respect your child's preparedness to debrief develops their emotional intelligence.

When you both are ready, ask about the pool story using this pattern: "What happened? What should have happened? How did you get out of the pool?" The goal is to have the child think through their actions. Ask questions only. Avoid lecturing, arguing, or trying to teach a lesson. Here are a few more questions that you could ask that will encourage your child's critical thinking:

- What happened? How did you get in the pool?
- Was there a way to avoid the pool?
- Did you drag someone in with you?
- How did you get out of the pool? Was that way effective?
- Now that you are out, do you need to fix anything or apologize to anyone?
- Were others affected by your swim? If so, what are you going to do to restore the relationship?
- Was anything broken? If so, what are you going to do to repair it?

What Not to Do When Those You Love Are Going for a Swim

Because we love our family, we don't want to see them struggling in their pool. Our hearts hurt for them, and we feel anxious watching them. No matter their age, here are five responses that are not helpful:

170

Pool Rules

- **Ignoring that they are in the pool.** In your discomfort, you continue your actions and act like nothing is happening around you. Raelynn saw this when she visited her boyfriend's family for Thanksgiving. His sister, home from college, started mumbling about not having the right brand of cereal for breakfast. Somehow, her sputtering turned into a full-blown meltdown. The rest of her family ignored her and chatted nervously about their dinner plans, walking on eggshells around her. "It was so weird," Raelynn said. "No one addressed that she flung a cereal box across the room."

- **Trying to give advice.** Asking someone, "The next time you find yourself in this situation, what are you going to do differently?" while they are still in their pool is unkind. Or, even worse, "Well, I hope that you learned . . ."

- **Arguing with them.** For example, if your sibling is upset about an acne breakout on her face, you say, "But look at you! You're pretty!"

- **Explaining their emotions to them.** Although naming emotions is a wonderful way to understand the pool, many times while a family member is still in the pool, it doesn't seem useful. For example, if your daughter just totaled her car and you say, "You are upset and tired," your words are likely to be more irritating than comforting.

- **Responding with factual data.** When you say, "If you look at just the exam pass rate for first-time takers, the CPA exam is only a 14 to 20 percent pass rate," it is not as helpful as you may think when someone has put in hours of preparation and feels deep disappointment at failing the test.

Although well-meaning, these responses are more about your need to make yourself feel better than to soothe the other person. Wait until they are out of the pool to discuss what happened with them.

you. Instead of trying to rescue them—to stop them from feeling a certain way or to coax them out of the pool—find a way that allows them to swim to the side of the pool. For example, you could reach them by offering your calm presence, saying, "I see that you are upset. Would it help if I just sat with you briefly?" Or you could throw a flotation device their way, like when a parent reminds a child of their coping strategies.

Some family members are compulsive divers. When someone is in their pool, they dive in to offer support. You may be overhelping when you find yourself doing more to help others out of their pool than they're doing for themselves. (Chapter 15 talks more about this.) Remember, everyone has the responsibility to get out of their own pool.

Pool Stories

Eventually, we all plunge into the pool. Emotionally healthy families encourage emotional expression and create an environment where feelings are acknowledged and accepted. They are allowed to experience a wide range of emotions and are supported as they find healthy ways to cope with them. So instead of working on preventing any slips or slides into the pool, we need to develop the ability to talk about the pool in a way that encourages growth and development.

Sharing pool stories, both positive and negative, is a way that families can talk about their big emotions, safely process them, and build a culture of shared understanding. Because individuals with ADHD may struggle to recall and retain emotional memories accurately, talking through this metaphor can increase their learning from emotional experiences. Pool stories have a predictable pattern: what led to you falling into the pool, what you used to get out of it, and what you can learn from it. Emotional intelligence is nurtured and empathy is cultivated when waterlogged events are discussed. Reflecting on how you engage the pool can help you make sense of your emotional processing.

While it's natural to experience a broad range of emotions, intense and rapid fluctuations in emotions (a jump into the pool) can be a source of confusion or distress for those around you. The pool metaphor provides a picture of how hyperarousal and hypoarousal affect us and those we love.

Although those with ADHD will still struggle with emotional dysregulation, impaired awareness, and impulsive responses, families who learn to process emotions provide each member a strong foundation of support. They actively listen to one another, validate each other's feelings, and offer empathy and understanding. There is a genuine concern for each other's well-being and a willingness to provide comfort and reassurance during challenging times.

If you are in an ADHD family, remember that the only brain you can manage is yours. Whether or not you have ADHD, you can be the one in your family who develops the ability to regulate your behavior, emotions, and thoughts. Others can leap into their pool around you, but you don't need to join them.

14

GOOD MORNING, POISON SQUIRRELS

The 1970s punk rock band Poison Squirrel got its name from a funny incident involving one of the band members' families. His five-year-old child used to watch the children's television series *Romper Room*. Every morning, the preschooler heard the hostess begin the show with a cheerful greeting: "Good morning, poison squirrels." That misinterpretation inspired the band's unique name.

Every family has stories like those. Children mishear words like "boys and girls" and replace them with the oronym "poison squirrels." It's also amusing when children confuse concepts. When my daughter read her calendar on November 11, Veterans Day, she cautioned, "I don't think we are supposed to eat meat today," thinking it was vegetarian day. Mishearing words, misunderstanding concepts, and other communication glitches are funny when small children are involved. But they aren't always so amusing when adults experience a communication breakdown. Neurodiverse families can experience several issues that interfere with their ability to understand each other.

Effective Communication

I consciously practice effective communication during my work-day. I try to listen carefully and focus on my client's point of view. I come home tired and leave my thoughtful communication skills next to my boots and coat at the door. Some nights after work, a phrase like, "Well, that's a dumb idea," slips out, and sometimes I don't even catch my error because I think the idea is a really dumb one. I haven't taken the time to filter my response to something like, "Can you tell me more about what you're thinking?" I forget to use my well-developed communication skills.

Parents often have a similar experience with their children. Teachers go out of their way to tell parents what a well-behaved and helpful child they have. The parents nod and accept the compliment while remembering their child's regular after-school meltdowns. In fact, one parent recalls their daughter's breakdown just yesterday on their way home because her brother drank the last box of cherry juice. Instead of using her words, "I'm angry about this," as she may have done in school with her teacher, she communicated her annoyance with a meltdown. The parents comfort each other by reminding themselves that they created a place where their daughter is completely comfortable being herself and that she knows how to behave at school. "It's exhausting to experience our children's emotions with them, but at least they know they are safe with me," the parent recently told me. "It's especially frustrating when I know that they can do better. But then I need to remember that they had to hold it together at school."

Unfortunately, we all save our best behavior—and communication—for coworkers, clients, and classmates. Interestingly, we often find ourselves practicing better communication skills with individuals who are more distant from us or not as emotionally close to us, which may seem ironic. This is because we don't feel as safe. The formality in these relationships prompts our

Are you practicing effective communication with your family? Under "Self," place a check mark next to which of the following you do regularly. Under "Family," place a check mark if your family would agree.

Self	Family	
☐	☐	I notice household issues, and I discuss them with a family member from their point of view.
☐	☐	When I talk to a family member, I put myself in their shoes.
☐	☐	I can tell when someone in my family doesn't understand what I'm saying.
☐	☐	When talking to people, I pay attention to their body language (facial expressions, hand movements, etc.).
☐	☐	I try to detect the mood of a family member by looking at them as we converse.
☐	☐	I use my polite voice when I disagree with someone.
☐	☐	I manage to express my ideas clearly.
☐	☐	I admit there are specific issues we may never agree upon.
☐	☐	I am willing to consider other options for solving a problem.

nervous system to help us be more attentive listeners, observe nonverbal cues, and let others express themselves fully.

Look at the items in the sidebar and inventory your interactions with family members. This inventory can help you become aware of any communication shortcomings or lapses. If you are ready for a challenge, ask a family member to review the list and give you feedback.

Quirky Communication Patterns

While communication can present challenges for everyone, those with ADHD encounter communication difficulties more frequently than the average population. These difficulties can be attributed to several reasons. Still, it's essential to clarify that these quirks are not a result of a lack of respect for others. Many of them stem from issues with executive functions. ADHD may cause distractions and forgetfulness, making it challenging to maintain focus during conversations. Consequently, some people with ADHD may struggle with social skills, such as taking turns in discussions, reading social cues, or understanding social norms, which impacts their ability to engage in meaningful interactions.

Not every person with ADHD will experience all these communication issues, and the severity may vary among individuals. However, research indicates that people with ADHD may exhibit communication problems that could be perceived as egocentric behaviors.[1] Communication issues can significantly impact relationships and overall quality of life because communication is vital to various relationships, including family, romantic connections, friendships, and professional associations. When communication becomes problematic, the relationship may suffer, making it necessary to address these difficulties to preserve the relationship.

Short-Term and Working Memory Issues

Do you forget essential conversations or decisions you made? Do you frequently say, "I forgot what I was going to say"? Do you forget what someone is saying—even when you are still conversing? Do you say the same thing more than once in a conversation? Do you find it difficult to retrieve the word you want? Do you find managing multiple pieces of information in a conversation challenging? If you answered yes to many of these questions, short-term and working memory deficits associated with ADHD may significantly affect your communication, interfering with your ability to receive and convey your thoughts effectively. Many of us have difficulties remembering information, instructions, or conversations. We frequently experience forgetfulness during conversations, and we struggle to retain important information and lose track of intended points or critical details mentioned by others.

Arguments start in families with someone accusing another, "You never told me that!" Or we shame another family member by saying, "I've already told you that." This can be frustrating for individuals with ADHD and their communication partners. Our family members without ADHD may even develop the false belief that we just don't care enough to listen.

We also may have difficulty getting information out. Because the mental filing system for organizing information in the brain is less efficient for ADHD adults, retrieving words or ideas from long-term memory is often more complex.[2] In addition, there are usually ten ideas fighting for airtime. We tend to have more frequent pauses, verbal fillers, or incorrect words as we try to retrieve what we want to say. The limited working memory capacity, which lasts only ten to fifteen seconds, further compounds the issue. Thoughts within our reach slip away when we are distracted by anything in our environment. Others may find it challenging to understand our message.

As you speak, watch the other person's response; if you notice that they react differently than you expected based on what you wanted to say, ask them kindly to tell you what they think you said. This might sound like, "I feel like something isn't right. Maybe I wasn't clear. Could you tell me what you heard me say or what you think I mean?"

As if the difficulty receiving and getting out messages wasn't hazardous enough for us, some of us have problems processing information during discussions. Many of my clients have processing issues that make it difficult to follow a conversation or grasp complex ideas. Finn explains it this way: "It's like I'm watching a basketball game. The ball is moving so fast that I can't follow it. And I lose track of who is on each team. It's all a blur." Even though Finn has a higher-than-average IQ, his processing speed is slower than the speed of many conversations.

Kaylee has found a way to explain this to others lightheartedly, saying, "Could you repeat what you just said? I'm not a fast listener." She tells me that people are usually happy to repeat their words and wait while she writes down the information. "It helps me with my family who doesn't have ADHD. I can remind them that I'm a slow listener."

In addition to memory-related challenges, other communication quirks hamper effective communication and impact our ability to actively listen, process incoming information, and formulate appropriate responses during dynamic conversations. The following are ten quirks I see when I work with families.

Quirk 1: The ADHD Mind Wandering during a Conversation

We may struggle with maintaining attention during conversations. We become distracted by external stimuli or internal thoughts, causing us to miss important details or lose track of the conversation. Then we catch ourselves and blurt, "Wait, what?"

Addressing the quirk: A tip that appears to work effectively to solve this kind of communication problem in families is to agree on a signal word. For example, families decide to gently remind each other if they notice they are wandering. That way, they know that they need to return to the previous topic. Choose a word that sounds funny to your family, like onomatopoeia, sassafras, or collywobbles, because it will get their attention.

Quirk 2: Telling Stories from the Inside Out

Sequencing ideas can be challenging for those with ADHD.[3] When telling a story, I often begin somewhere in the middle and tell it from both ends. Oh, and then there are the tangents that I wander into.

Addressing the quirk: I don't usually address this in others because I want them to tell the story any way they want to. I assume that I'll eventually figure it out. But I try to address the quirk in myself. Before I tell a story, I ask myself, "Why am I telling the story? What happened first, second, etc.?" I often don't catch myself and launch into an epic tale. When I'm speaking to someone without ADHD, I say, "Oops! I forgot you're probably listening to the order in which it happened. Let me back up."

Quirk 3: Tangents and More Tangents

ADHD brains often prefer divergent thinking, in which everything is connected.[4] This means that as you speak, you think of other related ideas and issues. For example, you're talking to your dad and sister about your son's stellar baseball game and remember a quote you read from Babe Ruth. You share the quote and how it relates to the *Spider-Man* movie you saw. And before you know it, you are discussing climate and environmental issues.

Addressing the quirk: Although I particularly enjoy this quirk because I find it interesting, others may not. Some people feel disoriented and confused with too many tangents. If the conversation needs resolution, focus on the outcome. At the very least, provide a turn signal in the discussion that indicates you are changing the course of the conversation. A brief segue like, "When we finish talking about this, I'd like to address . . ." allows your listener to follow your thought.

Quirk 4: Distracted Instead of Listening

Getting distracted is quite common, and before you realize it, you might find yourself not fully engaged in the conversation. Even a brief lapse in attention can cause you to miss essential information or the main point being discussed. This can lead others to believe you're disinterested or intentionally not paying attention.

Addressing the quirk: Make eye contact when someone's speaking to you. Focus on the discussion and read nonverbal communication cues like facial expressions. Try to minimize distractions. For example, don't look at your phone. You might put it in your pocket or purse or turn it face down. Eliminate your unnecessary tech alerts because although you would love to know how many people responded to your Instagram post, it can wait. If for some reason you can't focus, offer a solution, like finding a quieter place to talk. Or if you can't process what is being said because you are focused on another activity, simply say, "I can't give this my full attention now. Can we talk in half an hour?"

Quirk 5: Walking Out Mid-Conversation

I'm not talking about walking off during an argument. I'm talking about wandering off while someone is speaking. This just happened in our house. I was talking to my husband about a household detail. I was mid-sentence when he looked away and walked toward the back door. I turned to my non-ADHD daughter, confused. "Ummm, he just walked away."

She shrugged. "You both do that."

I had no idea I did that too.

Later when I asked my husband why he walked away, he said, "Oh, I think I know what you're talking about. Yep, I forgot to turn off the pool pump. It's like my brain was flooded with only that idea."

Addressing the quirk: This is a problematic quirk to catch on your own. If a family member does this, please don't assume a motive of disrespect. Give them the benefit of the doubt, ask about the quirk, and pick up the conversation when possible. I wrote a note on my calendar about the details I was discussing so that I could talk about them later with my husband.

Quirk 6: Starting a Conversation without Context

Sometimes we begin a discussion in our head and then finish it aloud, confusing those around us.

Addressing the quirk: We usually need to catch this habit after we've started a conversation. After reading the confusion on another person's face, Billi smiles and jokes about her quirk. "Since you can't read my mind, how about I tell you what led me to say this?" In addition to displaying self-awareness, saying this helps her listener follow her logic.

Quirk 7: Talking Only about Topics That Interest You

Those of us with ADHD may struggle to sustain attention and engagement during conversations, especially if the subject is not highly stimulating to us. When we make the error of talking only about the things that are emotionally stimulating to us, we are being egocentric and not considering what others may find important or interesting.[5]

Addressing the quirk: A trick I've learned is to engage my curiosity, a trait many of us have in abundance. Let's say that someone brings up sports. Now, I hate talking about most things related to sports. I don't care about players, games, or team trends. I used to try to change the topic to something I was interested in until I realized it was selfish. The other person cared about sports. So when someone says, "U of M just lost their quarterback," I engage my curiosity. *Why is this a significant statement?* I wonder, then ask aloud, "What do you think will happen because of that?"

Quirk 8: Interrupting

During a conversation, we may have an important question. Or we have a brilliant idea (at least in our perception). If we try to hold that thought for a moment, we will lose it, so we throw it out in the middle of the conversation. People with ADHD frequently blurt comments or interrupt others without considering the appropriate timing or social context.[6] Although we intend to add to the conversation, others can perceive this as rude.

This is perhaps my greatest communication challenge. The more interested I am in a discussion, the greater my tendency to interrupt.

Addressing the quirk: I return to my values. I remind myself that I care for and respect the person talking and want to slow down and hear what they say. Sometimes when I am on the phone with family members, I put myself on mute to fully listen. Although they cannot hear me, I can still interrupt them and it doesn't interfere with their train of thought.

Another helpful strategy is to teach yourself to ask questions after you've spoken a couple of sentences, giving the other person a chance to share their thoughts. Additionally, silently repeating what the other person says can help you focus on listening rather than dominating the conversation. It's essential to be aware of how often you interrupt others, as doing so repeatedly can be perceived as rude, even if it stems from a fear of forgetting something important. Setting a goal to limit interruptions during a conversation can be beneficial.

Quirk 9: Talking Too Much

Talking too much can be a challenge for individuals dealing with ADHD symptoms, as they might lose sight of the balance in a conversation. Particularly when discussing a topic they are passionate about, they may dominate the conversation, unintentionally disregarding the other person's input and making them feel unheard. Unfortunately, dominating makes us look self-centered. I don't know much about this in my life, but I have read that it's an issue.

Addressing the quirk: A simple yet effective solution is to consciously practice taking breaks after speaking a few sentences. Allowing the other person time to respond and actively listening to their answers without thinking about your reply can foster more balanced communication. Asking questions and repeating the other person's words can also demonstrate genuine interest and help prevent interruptions. By adopting these strategies, individuals with ADHD can create more inclusive and engaging conversations while avoiding the tendency to dominate the conversation.

Quirk 10: Thinking about What You Will Say and Forgetting to Listen

When we aren't interrupting, we may think about what we will declare as someone speaks. When we are formulating a response, we aren't really listening.

Addressing the quirk: Teach yourself to ask questions. Bonnie plays a game in her mind. "Before I respond to my teenager, I ask two or three questions to show that I'm listening. It helps me slow down, be less reactive, and stay present in the conversation."

Can you add to this quirky communication list? Of course you can. Every family has its own set of peccadilloes when interacting with each other. What communication quirks do you see in your family?

One of my quirks is speaking in genres. My husband was puzzled for years when I said I was going to Home Depot but came home with bags from Lowe's. When we discussed it, I explained, "When I say Home Depot, I mean any big-box home improvement store." Now when I announce that I will go shopping for a house project, he asks, "Blue or orange?"

Be open with each other about the quirks you experience and how they affect you. Develop strategies together as you discuss the peculiarities in a nonjudgmental way. Additionally, individuals with ADHD may develop coping strategies and improve communication skills with appropriate support like coaching and therapy. The goal of family communication is to foster understanding and connection and not to debate the peculiarities in your conversation.

15

MONKEY CHATTER

Seven-year-old Jonathan and I played with small beanbag monkeys on my office floor. We had already named a few of them: Disorganized Derek, Angry Andrew, and Impatient Iggy. When I asked which of his ADHD monkeys talks to the others, he quickly ascertained that Impatient Iggy tells Disorganized Derek that he doesn't have time to put his shoes in the hallway basket. As he demonstrated the conversation between the two floppy animals, he stopped and said, "My mom's Anxious Amy monkey talks to my monkeys too." Jonathan was already aware of the contagious nature of anxiety.

As I picked up one of the monkeys, I looked at him and said, "That's interesting. Can we pretend this monkey is your mom's Anxious Amy? What does she say to your monkeys?"

He shrugged, pushed up his glasses, and gazed at the new monkey. "Well, her monkey doesn't say words. It's more like 'Eek-aak-eek! AH! AH!'" he said, bouncing the monkey up and down.

"And then how do your monkeys react?" I asked.

He responded by scooping up his menagerie, throwing them in the air, and laughing at his silliness. His actions show what

185

happens when anxiety enters the family system: it upsets our ADHD monkeys.

In chapter 3, you named your ADHD monkeys, and you learned that your monkeys interact with each other, creating a cacophonous conversation in your head. They either fight with one another like Disorganized Derek and Perfect Penny do, creating arguments over how clean your bedroom should be, or they join forces to make a compelling emotional case, like when Rejection-Sensitive Rachel and Critical Calvin agree that you shouldn't apply for that promotion because you are not good enough.

Did you know that our family members' monkeys also talk to one another? Monkey chatter isn't restricted to our own heads. My monkeys affect your monkeys, and your monkeys affect mine. And our monkey malarky often leads to panicky chaos in a family.

This chapter explores three ways that anxiety affects our family system. Before we look at the communal aspects of stress, we first need to appreciate the purpose of anxiety and how it affects us as individuals.

Individual Anxiety

Anxiety serves the crucial purpose of alerting and motivating us to avoid real dangers. Fear and excitement both stem from the same chemical reaction in our bodies. Adrenaline stimulates the sympathetic nervous system and prepares us for action. For instance, feeling anxious when we are in danger of falling off a cliff keeps us safe. Similarly, experiencing anxiety before an important test can act as a driving force for action, like studying. When we work with anxiety constructively by viewing it as an uncomfortable yet natural aspect of life, we can gain new tools to cope with it.

We all have a version of Anxious Amy in our amygdala, and she alerts us when she senses risk. However, those of us with ADHD tend to have an anxiety monkey that doesn't classify dangers according to their appropriate level. She regularly confuses small threats with significant risks. When we feel the crushing weight of our household to-do list and worry that it will never get done, Anxious Amy tells us this is a significant threat and we should be very agitated. And when we add to this our beautiful imaginations and divergent thinking, we have overly alert, overactive, and creative Anxious Amys. Oh, the horrible things she can imagine.

Although anxiety itself is not inherently harmful, it can feel distressing. In some cases, it might become disordered. In this state, anxiety interferes with or takes control of our lives, making it challenging to function in various areas such as work, school, and other aspects of life.

Anxiety becomes disordered when one of two conditions arises:

1. Feeling as if you are in danger even when you are safe
2. Struggling to perform daily tasks

My client Sandy harbored an irrational fear of clicking sounds, like the sound a gas stove makes when you turn it on. Merely being in a room with the sound would trigger intense anxiety and profuse sweating. Although the clicking sound posed no threat to Sandy, her body would respond as if she was facing genuine danger. This mismatch between perceived and actual safety characterizes disordered anxiety.

Anxiety is also problematic when it starts interfering with your ability to lead an everyday life. If anxiety or your attempts to avoid it leads to things like avoiding school, taking frequent sick leaves from work, isolating yourself from friends, or becoming housebound, it's time to seek help. Talking with a therapist will be essential to your growth if either of the above conditions is present.

Family Anxiety

Now that we understand a few aspects of individual anxiety, let's look at how it can affect a family.

Nina's monkey Overwhelmed Oscar came out one night. "I just hate math. I hate homework. I hate school!" she said as she flopped her head on the table. Instead of addressing her daughter's frustration and overwhelm, Abigail responded with her own anxious monkey. Her thoughts raced to find a solution to the problem. *Is she okay? I don't want her to feel bad. Should I tell her that she doesn't need to do it? What should I do to fix this? Should I call the teacher? Should I move her to another school?* The anxious monkey wanted to make everyone's big emotions go away and restore a sense of calm. She wanted Abigail to fix Nina's problem so that both of them would feel better.

Nina's Anxious Amy picked up on her mother's response and thought, *Mom seems upset. Maybe homework really is dangerous.* Now, besides feeling frustrated with her homework, she also felt anxious. Due to their unique brain wiring, Nina and many others with ADHD are particularly prone to detecting and reacting to another person's anxious demeanor.

Anxiety can be contagious. Families everywhere respond to each other's stress in unhelpful ways, creating more issues. Anxiety in families is often like dropping a rock in a calm pond, creating a series of concentric circles that expand outward from the point of disturbance. Family anxiety is the diffusion of fear, concern, unease, or nervousness rippling across an entire family unit. ADHD monkeys sense the disturbance and become vigilant. Then they initiate their own individual reactions. Before we know it, we have monkey mayhem.

When you are around someone who is anxious, remember to calm yourself first. When you are calm, acknowledge the person's anxiety by saying something like, "Hey, I see that you are anxious (or worried, concerned, or stressed), and I'd like to help." That validates the person's feelings and offers support. Talking openly about anxious thoughts and how they affect your family members can be a way to release their grip.

Suppose the family is not actively addressing the individual's anxiety and instead ignoring it or transferring it to others. In that case, the anxiety will likely permeate the entire family and worsen for the person from whom it originated.

The rest of this chapter focuses on three specific ways anxiety can drip into your family: same-event anxiety, accommodation, and chronic culture of anxiety. Let's unpack each of them so you can learn to successfully navigate some of these difficulties.

Same-Event Anxiety

Same-event anxiety is when everyone is anxious about the same thing. Usually it is sparked by an event, an experience, or a time in a family's life, like moving to a new town, divorce, loss of a family pet, adoption, a new member of the family, illness, or injury. Although everyone responds to the same source, individuals express their unease differently because Anxious Amy partners with other monkeys to express concerns.

Barb starts dating again after a divorce. As she gets ready to go out, Anxious Amy begins nervously chattering. "You've been out of the dating world for quite a while. Are you really ready?" While Barb looks in the mirror, applying her mascara, Helpless Hannah responds to Anxious Amy, reminding Barb that her life already feels hard. "Is it even worth it?"

Her children, Jace and Denzel, also feel the anxiety related to this new time in their lives. Anxious Amy recruits Angry Andrew to come to ten-year-old Jace's rescue, and he starts acting out as Barb is getting ready for her date.

Thirteen-year-old Denzel responds differently. Mopey Mike and Avoidant Ava step in to pacify Anxious Amy's alarm. Denzel sits quietly in his room, playing video games on his computer.

Everyone communicates anxiety differently, even though it's from the same source—in this case, the uncertainty around Barb's dating. Some people, like Jace, seem to amplify the anxiety, and others, like Denzel, seem to absorb it.

Same-event anxiety occurs when a change or transition leaves you grieving a loss or fearful about the future. It is helpful for the family to discuss changes and, when possible, what to expect. Talking about what your family is experiencing when you are going through a transition—whether it's exciting, like an adoption, or distressing, like an illness—goes a long way toward normalizing the anxiety that naturally occurs with any change. Taking leadership in moments like this might sound like, "This is a change for all of us, and we have different emotions about it. And we might feel nervous having these big emotions." Then discuss the adjustment, what to expect, and the process of accepting the change. When the tension is palpable, you can say, "We all feel anxious about this. That's okay. Let's talk about it."

Accommodation

The second way anxiety affects families is through accommodation, where fear is spread through one anxious individual into the family, and the rest of the family adapts to it. Accommodation is any change a family member makes to their behavior to help another family member prevent or lessen their anxiety. Sometimes it can be helpful, but many times it is not.

Parmer's work environment was complicated due to recent cutbacks. Anxious Amy jumped into action, worried about the possibility of other changes. Would Parmer's job description change? Would he need to go to a different team? Would he lose his job? At home, he was cranky. He slammed cupboard doors while mumbling about the lack of organization in the kitchen and snapped at the children when he saw a forgotten blanket fort in the living room. His family could sense Anxious Amy. They began to tiptoe around him without understanding what they were doing.

"He's just in a stressful time," his wife explained to the kids, and they began to accommodate his distress. They attempted to ensure Anxious Amy wasn't aroused at home to avoid upsetting Parmer.

These tiny changes and maneuvers typically come from a caring and loving place, where family members want to ensure their loved one's happiness or the absence of distress. As in our earlier homework dilemma, Abigail's first instinct was accommodating her daughter's angst. She wanted to respond to Nina's irritation by trying to rescue her and eliminate the source of stress instead of helping her master new strategies.

The terms "rescue" and "mastery" are often used to describe two different approaches or mindsets toward challenges and problems. People in the rescue mindset may be uncomfortable with uncertainty, difficulty, or failure, and they seek to avoid these feelings by seeking help or avoiding the challenge altogether. This mindset can lead to dependency on others for solutions. While the rescue cycle can provide short-term relief, it may not lead to long-term skill development or personal growth because individuals do not fully engage with the problem or take ownership of the solution.

> Accommodation is any change a family member makes to their behavior to help another family member prevent or lessen their anxiety.

Even though Abigail initially responded with her own anxiety and her first thoughts were to accommodate, she caught herself. Taking a deep breath, she talked to her own Anxious Amy, reminding her that her daughter was a capable child and could figure out how to manage her academic frustrations. She remembered the mastery mindset she had been practicing from parent coaching. This mindset fosters skill development, resilience, and personal growth over time. It encourages individuals to build their competence and confidence in handling various situations. Abigail walked calmly toward her daughter and said, "Hmm. It sounds like you are frustrated."

When I first learned about accommodation years ago, I couldn't believe what I was hearing. Wasn't I supposed to show love and care to my family by making their lives easier? Wasn't I supposed to worry and fuss about people I loved? I couldn't believe how selfish this theory sounded. I confused showing anxiety for showing love. When family members convey, "I have anxiety for you, therefore

I love you," relationships are more complex. Instead, I learned to show confidence in my family member's ability to figure things out. Sure, I would always be there as a resource, but I allowed them to grow instead of attempting to do things for them.

Gradually, I learned to ask myself questions about whether my helping was harming those I loved. Reflect on the following questions to determine whether accommodation plays a significant role in your family dynamics.

Do I engage in anxiety-driven behaviors? Are you actively involved in behaviors that aim to alleviate your family member's anxiety? Do you go to great lengths to ensure their comfort? Parmer's wife didn't mention that their twenty-year-old furnace was acting up, even though she worried it might stop working. In fact, she tried not to bring up any bad news. She completely took over anything relating to the children—homework, meals, and bedtime all became her sole responsibility—in hopes of avoiding his anxious outbursts.

Do I alter my routine or schedule because of my family member's anxiety? Are you making significant changes to your daily life because of your family member's anxiety, therefore affecting your life and your children, siblings, extended family, or friends? Maybe you avoid family vacations due to a family member's fear of flying or cancel date nights to ensure a parent is always at home with the child. Reflect on whether these modifications have become so commonplace that they seem normal despite their impact. Consider how anxiety-driven behaviors affect your life and responsibilities, such as arriving late for work, taking leave from work, or sacrificing personal time for your family member's needs. Ask yourself if you would allocate the same amount of time and effort if your child were not anxious. If your answer is no, it may indicate that you are accommodating too much or in an unhealthy manner.

Are my accommodation behaviors healthy or unhealthy? Some level of accommodation is natural and necessary for supporting your family members. But challenge yourself by reflecting on why you are helping them. Are you accommodating because it is easier for you if you do? If so, work with a therapist to determine why you do this and how you can create better boundaries. Are you accommodating out of your past experiences or previous trauma? If so, a therapist can help guide you to transformational thinking (chapter 8).

If your family member is an adult, trust that they are capable, creative, and resourceful and that it is their responsibility to manage themselves. If your family member is a child, help them see difficulties as opportunities for growth and learning. Encourage them to persist in overcoming obstacles. Model how to be more comfortable with discomfort, failure, and setbacks because you view them as essential components of the learning process. When you help them build their competence and confidence in handling various situations, you support a mastery mindset, allowing them to tackle challenges independently.

When some of my clients realize they have been accommodating in harmful ways, they feel angry at themselves and their family members. I encourage them not to overcorrect and angrily withdraw all support. Instead, I ask them to change their mindset from rescuing their family member to supporting them as they develop mastery.

Chronic Culture of Anxiety

All families experience acute stress in response to temporary challenges or life transitions. The third way that anxiety affects families is when it permeates the family culture and affects how everyone interacts. Some families also contend with a continuous state of chronic anxiety. Chronic stress stems from ongoing

Anxiety helps us to gauge danger, and sometimes it is normal to feel anxiety.

reactivity within the family and revolves around perceived or imagined threats.

Psychiatrist Murray Bowen developed a systems theory of the family, which says that families operate as emotional units, where the emotional well-being of each member is interconnected with that of others in the family. When families affected by ADHD experience heightened emotional intensity, connection increases. People often say about their emotionally fused families, "Sure, we fight a lot and we're loud, but we love each other!" Being interconnected isn't good or bad. Instead, it is part of a delicate balance.

HEALTHY MIX OF CONNECTEDNESS AND PERSONAL FREEDOM

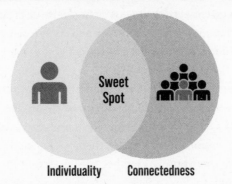

Individuality   Connectedness

Every family must find the right mixture of individuality and togetherness. In families with low levels of chronic anxiety, a healthy dose of connectedness coexists with ample freedom for individuals to express their true selves. Conversely, in families coping with high levels of chronic anxiety, individuals encounter heightened togetherness, leading to minimal emotional boundaries between them. While togetherness can yield positive feelings, its value emerges when paired with individuality. Without this crucial pairing, the capacity for individuals to pursue their personal journeys becomes constrained. If your family has a culture of anxiety, you'll see an emotional tug-of-war where some of your family members overfunction while others underfunction.

Overfunctioning. The Disney movie *Encanto* is an excellent example of overfunctioning and underfunctioning. Set in Colombia, *Encanto* is about the intergenerational Madrigal family, whose members each have a miraculous gift to use for the good of the community. Isabela is gifted with spreading beauty wherever she goes. Luisa is super strong and can handle everyone's problems. Juliet understands what needs to be healed in a person and can bake a unique item for them to eat and be healed. In their effort to bless their community, they end up overfunctioning, feeling stressed and overwhelmed. Isabela is saddled with ensuring everything is happy and peaceful wherever she goes. Luisa finds carrying everyone's problems exhausting. Juliet grows weary of healing everyone's afflictions. The problem is that they are overfunctioning. They believe they are responsible for the emotional and physical burdens of the entire village.

When someone overfunctions, they assume others' responsibilities or sometimes experience others' emotions. As a result, people around them don't need to take responsibility for themselves because the overfunctioning one does it for them.

Many family members discuss their overfunctioning with me. Instead of resolving their own fears, insecurities, and anxieties, they follow their urge to manage, help, and change their loved ones. Those who overfunction tend to be fixers and problem-solvers. They give advice, rescue, take over, micromanage, and get into other people's business. It's no surprise they show up in my office depleted and resentful. Overfunctioning isn't the answer for you or the person you are trying to help.

If you have been overfunctioning, it's time to increase your threshold for others' pain instead of trying to remedy their discomfort. It's difficult to watch those you love so dearly in a challenging position, but you need to allow them the space to grow. You can help someone develop a mastery mindset instead of a rescue mindset by offering support, guidance, and encouragement, empowering them to take ownership of their challenges and develop the skills and resilience needed to overcome them independently. Help the individual reflect on their current mindset and problem-solving approaches. Ask open-ended questions that prompt them to consider how they typically respond to challenges. Create an environment where they feel safe taking risks and making mistakes. This reduces the fear of failure and encourages experimentation and growth.

Underfunctioning. Encanto also provides us with examples of characters who are underfunctioning. When people underfunction, they allow others to think, act, or feel for them. Camillo is a shape-shifter who can become like anyone around him. He can lose himself to be just like anyone else. Another underfunctioning character is Pepa. Her mood affects the weather. When she's happy, the world is sunny. When she's sad, it rains. When she's angry, everyone is pelted in a massive storm. The family and village manage Pepa's emotions for her, which doesn't allow her to develop her own strategies.

In stressful situations, underfunctioning people tend to get less competent. They invite others to take over and often become the focus of family gossip, concern, and worry.

Once you've identified that you tend to rely on external help or avoid challenges, you'll want to transition to a mastery mindset. Continue to monitor and acknowledge when you are in a rescue mindset. Pay attention to the situations or challenges that trigger this response. Understand that seeking help or feeling uncomfortable in the face of challenges is perfectly normal. Avoid self-blame and accept that everyone encounters difficulties. Shift your perspective on discomfort and failure. Instead of avoiding problems, view them as opportunities for growth and learning. Understand that mastery requires overcoming challenges. Proactively seek out information, resources, and learning opportunities related to your challenges. This could involve reading, taking courses, or seeking advice from experts.

Although Anxious Amy wants to help you resolve issues that challenge you or your family, she may mislead you. Recognize how anxiety plays a role in your family's functioning by stepping back from immediate emotional reactions and observing patterns of same-event anxiety, accommodation, and a chronic culture of anxiety. When you do, you can respond more calmly and thoughtfully. You can encourage better communication as you become more aware of what's causing tension, learn to manage those challenges, and have open conversations about the underlying issues. When anxiety decreases, family members are more likely to work together smoothly, creating an environment that supports personal growth and positive relationships.

16

UNREGULATED EMPATHY

I don't mean to be rude, but . . ."

My stomach twisted as Simon Cowell from *American Idol* spoke. My girls and I watched the singing competition on the couch while snacking on popcorn. Watching Simon's unsparing, blunt appraisal of each contestant's talent, personality, or physical appearance was emotionally and physically taxing. I made sympathetic sounds and said things like, "Oh, that was too mean," or, "This makes me so sad."

Evidently, my children didn't appreciate my compassion because they challenged me. One daughter tried to reason with me. "Aw, come on, Mom. They *were* bad. Even they know it."

Another daughter tried to make me feel better. "They are on television. They're getting their fifteen minutes of fame."

Finally, my laments became too much for one of them. She stood up, exclaimed, "Your empathy is wrecking everything!" and stormed off.

At the time, I didn't understand much about ADHD or why I was so sensitive to another person's feelings. *Isn't it good that I care so deeply about people's feelings? Doesn't it help me be a better person? To be a better parent?* I reasoned. As I have learned over time, and hopefully you'll begin to see in this chapter, empathy is a complex phenomenon with a few snares.

Three Types of Empathy

For all of us, empathy can be an incredible asset that allows us to understand and share the feelings of others. It's like a bridge as we relate with their joys, sorrows, and perspectives. Our capacity for empathy has been linked to many positive outcomes, including improved emotional well-being, more robust social connections, and better overall health. Researchers have identified three distinct but interconnected types of empathy: emotional, cognitive, and compassionate.

Emotional Empathy

Emotional empathy, also known as affective empathy, is a component of empathy that involves the ability to share and vicariously experience the emotions of others. When someone has emotional empathy, they can "feel with" another person, connecting with that individual and understanding the emotional state they are in. Emotional empathy is valuable because it facilitates emotional bonds, supportive relationships, and a deeper understanding of others' experiences.

Emotional empathy tends to be an automatic and instinctive reaction. Those with high emotional empathy unconsciously mirror the emotional expressions and body language of those they interact with. Reflecting emotions back to someone helps build rapport and emotional connection with them. When faced with someone else's feelings, a person with emotional empathy immediately feels a similar emotional response without conscious effort. Some people are sympathetic criers, meaning they cry when others around them cry. Others might be sympathetic sneezers, where they sneeze when others do. Many clients tell me that if they see a video of someone getting injured, they feel it in their body. Emotional empathy is feeling with another person.

Cognitive Empathy

Think of cognitive empathy as the nerdy cousin of emotional empathy. It is more studious and relies on perspective-taking and interpretation. It goes beyond simply feeling the emotions someone is experiencing and delves into understanding that person's underlying mental state. People using cognitive empathy can "walk in others' shoes" to understand that different individuals may have unique thoughts, beliefs, and emotions based on their personal experiences, cultural backgrounds, and individual characteristics. Individuals using cognitive empathy tend to be more perceptive and precise in understanding what others are going through. Unlike emotional empathy, which involves sharing and feeling others' emotions, cognitive empathy allows individuals to understand others' experiences without being overwhelmed by their feelings. This detachment can be beneficial in maintaining emotional well-being while still being empathetic.

Compassionate Empathy

Compassionate empathy, also known as empathic concern, is a specific type of empathy that involves not only understanding and sharing the emotions of others (emotional empathy) but also feeling a deep sense of concern and a genuine desire to alleviate their suffering or promote their well-being. Unlike emotional empathy, which can be passive and even egocentric, compassionate empathy motivates individuals to provide assistance, comfort, or support to those in need.

The importance of using these three forms of empathy—emotional, cognitive, and compassionate—lies in their combined ability to enhance our interpersonal skills, foster healthier relationships, and promote empathy-driven positive behavior. The three types of empathy balance our perspective and responses. When they are not balanced, we experience the downsides of empathy.

Empathy Snares

As you have already learned, many of us with ADHD have problems with emotional self-regulation. Generally, when it comes to emotions, motivations, and actions, we are often like an off-on toggle switch. Many of us also have difficulty managing our emotional empathy. We are either engulfed in others' feelings or out of sync with their pain. We are most likely to show empathy in one of two settings: On (an intense empathetic response; a passionate, fixated, highly motivated approach to feeling with another person) or Off (little or no emotion; disinterest or little thought).

Emily's empathy switch was stuck in the On position. She was overwhelmed by profound sadness about her friend's divorce. Her persistent sadness, changes in appetite, and sleep disturbances affected her performance at work. Her family noticed that Emily's focus on her friend's situation led to a lack of concentration, forgetfulness, and an increased inability to make decisions. When you have ADHD, it is easy to lose yourself in your emotions about another person's emotions.

Others seem to have their empathy switch stuck in the Off position. When I asked Melania how her mother was doing after chemotherapy, she said, "Oh, that. She blames everything on her breast cancer. I'm getting sick of it." She told me her mother constantly complained about her health and ended with, "And she doesn't even have compassion for how hard I have been working."

Many of us with ADHD aren't even aware of our imbalanced empathy since we have used it as a coping strategy for so long. Because we have been reprimanded for missing details, not sitting still, or miscalculating arrival times, emotional empathy becomes a survival technique to help us manage the fallout of those errors. We use it to easily connect with people and be likable and more forgivable. Some of us have even learned the art of attuning to another's emotions to predict them and earn approval. For some of us, emotional empathy has become an issue of safety. We can be prepared to act if we can read and respond to situations.

I was an overempathizer for most of my life. I hated seeing others in pain, so I metaphorically jumped into the pool to join or try to rescue them. I believed that I could fix people and heal anything with compassion. I leaned heavily on my understanding that we're all human and have defects, so I needed to be patient with someone else's development.

Looking back, I realize I was missing a crucial piece. In addition to being patient with someone else's journey, I needed to remember that I am responsible for my personal growth and others are responsible for theirs. I needed to stop taking responsibility for others' emotional states and individual progress.

My emotional empathy assisted me as I parented my children, taught students, led staff, and coached clients. But it also allowed me to be taken advantage of and manipulated. I was too patient and empathetic with some people, acting as their emotional sponge. And sometimes I fell for their gaslighting, lying, sabotaging, and love bombing.

Now that you've read part 1 of this book, you can understand that my unregulated empathy stemmed from many emotional

Five Questions to Help Your Emotional Response

1. Am I absorbing others' emotions?
2. Am I overextending myself?
3. Do I feel overwhelmed?
4. Do I have difficulty saying no?
5. Am I managing my feelings while listening to someone else's?

errors and my lack of transformational thinking. I didn't need to become hard-hearted to regulate my empathy. Still, I did need to adopt some new beliefs and behaviors. I developed five questions that I posted on a large yellow sticky note on my computer as I learned to modify my emotional responses.

Question 1: Am I absorbing others' emotions?

When we have emotional empathy, we tend to take on the feelings and emotional experiences of those around us, often to an extent where we can't distinguish between our emotions and those of others.

Tim talked about his reliance on emotional empathy. "I feel other people's emotions so intensely. If they experience a loss, it's like I did too. It is so overwhelming." His deep level of empathy and sensitivity allowed him to connect profoundly with the emotional experiences of others, but he lost sight of how to regulate this ability. He was overwhelmed as the emotions of friends, family, and even strangers started to weigh heavily on his emotional state. He lost sight of his own feelings and well-being.

Achieving a balance between empathy and self-preservation becomes essential for effectively navigating life's situations.

Question 2: Am I overextending myself?

When we prioritize others' emotional needs over our own, it is often at the expense of our well-being.

Mila found herself prioritizing the emotional needs of her family, friends, and patients. She was the dependable rock within her family, offering an empathetic ear whenever needed. "My teens seem to only want to talk about their lives after eleven at night," she said with a laugh. "Even though it's past my bedtime, I want to be there for them."

Her steadfast empathy for others was seen in her profession and her community. As a family physician in a rural area, she knew that often her patients needed emotional and medical care. She believed that her concern should extend to the general community too. She volunteered at the local food bank and organized charity events to address the needs of those who might otherwise go unnoticed.

Though Mila's boundless empathy is a beautiful quality, it came at a cost to her well-being. At first, she noticed she was frequently fatigued and caught more colds. Gradually, she noticed that she felt depressed. Although she was usually upbeat and positive, she didn't have the energy to be happy. Her relentless focus on the feelings of others often came at the expense of her own mental, physical, and emotional well-being. Over time, the continuous self-sacrifice eroded her resilience, causing burnout, stress, and emotional exhaustion.

Finding a balance between offering support and safeguarding our emotional health is essential to maintaining lasting, healthy relationships and our personal well-being.

Question 3: Do I feel overwhelmed?

Unregulated empathy can lead to feelings of overwhelm, stress, and emotional exhaustion because we feel too much.

"I feel drained from my job," Kelly, a veterinarian, told me. She loved caring for the animals she treated and their families, providing emotional support and encouragement for pet parents concerned about their fur babies. She was such a good vet in part because she was great at connecting emotionally.

Kelly knew she was close to empathetic burnout and couldn't continue like she had been. "I just can't figure out how much I should care." She was devastated after losing an elderly dog during a dental cleaning. "When he died, I stood there and cried. My staff and I continued working, but inside, I felt immobile and sad. All I could think about was that poor, sweet dog and how his family would be so sad. All of my energy felt zapped the rest of the day." Kelly empathized with someone else's pain, sadness, and distress to the extent that it affected her well-being and emotional state. She told me she believed her frequent stomachaches and headaches were related to her feeling too much. She relied on one form of empathy—emotional empathy—which made the world feel like too much. Her empathetic distress left her feeling fully depleted, a type of burnout.

Sometimes we feel overwhelmed from watching the news. Incredibly saddened by the latest school shooting, Collin lay on his bed in his dorm room, stuck in his big emotions. He skipped his classes, didn't go to the dining hall with his friends at dinnertime, and couldn't find the energy to begin his homework. He imagined how he would feel if a shooting happened to him at school. He was trapped in his internal world and swirling big emotions. He almost failed his semester.

Working through our own emotional issues can make it challenging for us to shift our attention to the feelings of others—people like Collin's friend down the hall whose grandmother had just died. Collin couldn't be attentive to his friend's needs because he was swamped with his own emotions.

Managing our empathy is essential so we can continue functioning.

Question 4: Do I have difficulty saying no?

At times we might struggle to set healthy limits and have problems saying no to requests or emotional demands from others.

Ethan's thirty-six-year-old son, Eddie, lived with him and his wife after experiencing a bad breakup. Ethan was helping him with his bills and other expenses. He gave Eddie whatever he wanted. Eddie's older car needed work, so they decided to buy him a new one instead of fixing the old one. Ethan didn't see that he initially had difficulty saying no to his son and tried to assure me of his reasons. "He's had such a rough life. Bad things just seem to happen to him. He has a restraining order on him from his previous girlfriend and three citations for driving under the influence of alcohol. He can't find the right job." And the list of Eddie's sad circumstances continued. Ethan's unregulated empathy for his son wasn't encouraging Eddie to take responsibility for his life.

Emotional boundaries can feel harsh, but once you know the strength of saying no, they can protect you from people looking to take advantage of them.

Question 5: Am I managing my feelings while listening to someone else's?

Sometimes our empathy goes awry when we try to show compassion for another person but end up consumed by our own feelings. This frequently occurs when we want to connect with those we care about and share our stories of similar pain.

Ezra told his brother, Kai, that he'd just broken up with the person he'd thought he would marry. Kai understood those feelings and said, "Oh man, I am so sorry. That stinks." Then he launched into a story about his breakup and how shattered he was. He ended it with, "I know what you're feeling."

In our session, Ezra complained about his brother's apparent lack of empathy. "He doesn't know, does he? We're not the same person!" Kai attempted to empathize with his brother but focused on his own emotions as he spoke. Ezra felt that Kai was egocentric because he didn't show cognitive or compassionate empathy. To use the pool metaphor, it was like Ezra was in the pool and Kai said, "Hey! I'll also jump in and explore my big emotions about that topic."

Many family members like Ezra are puzzled when their loved ones underfunction in empathy. They know that they are capable of empathy, but it looks self-centered. As we empathize with someone, we may become preoccupied with our struggles, needs, or feelings about a situation.

Empathy is both beautiful and hazardous. Using the above five questions can help us regulate the intensity of our emotional empathy and learn not to rely solely on it. We can use the different kinds of empathy—emotional, cognitive, and compassionate—to intentionally shift our emotional responses and avoid feeling consumed by the emotions of others.

If you frequently find yourself in unregulated empathy, return to chapter 8 to regain your transformational mindset and to chapter 12 to stay out of the pool.[1]

17

TRIANGLES

Curt grimaces as he picks up the call. It's one of his brothers. "Hi, Doug," he says. His other brother, Joe, called earlier complaining about Doug, and Curt suspects Doug is calling to do the same about Joe. Three brothers—all in their forties and leaders in their family business—find themselves caught in a web of sibling rivalry and ongoing disagreements. Joe and Doug frequently clash, and Curt becomes the middleman, receiving phone calls from both brothers detailing their grievances. Joe believes that he is working harder than Doug. Doug is upset with Joe because the estate planning process is taking too much of his time. And Curt hears about it all.

This dynamic places Curt in a challenging position. Not only does he dedicate considerable time attempting to mediate his brothers' long-standing conflicts, but doing so is also emotionally draining. The stress becomes so overwhelming that he begins avoiding meetings where they are all together. It is also affecting other relationships. Curt's wife, Heather, told him that trying to make peace between his brothers affects their relationship because she feels like he is preoccupied when they are together. Curt is caught in a triangle. Doug and Joe have a strained relationship, and instead of working it out between the two of them, they complain to another person.

Making Triangles

Imagine this scenario: Alex is having difficulties in college and is afraid to share this with his parents. He confides in his older sibling, Jamie, about his struggles. Jamie, wanting to help and protect Alex, decides to talk to their parents without Alex's knowledge.

Let's examine the components of this problem. There is the initial tension that Alex is feeling with his parents regarding the academic challenges. Instead of directly addressing the issue with his parents, Alex indirectly involves Jamie, a third party. Their parents, unaware of Alex's academic struggles, receive information about them from Jamie. This is called triangulation. Families everywhere create triangles that can lead to misunderstandings and potentially unhealthy communication patterns. Alex may feel betrayed or invaded by Jamie, and the parents might feel blindsided or confused by the indirect communication.

Triangulation is a concept introduced by theorist Murray Bowen, who studied how families work across generations.[1] He explained that when two people in a relationship are facing difficulties, it's like a wonky stool with only two legs. When things are going well, these two people can handle their issues and support each other. But when they have problems or feel stressed because of changes, they might involve a third person, like adding another leg to the stool, to help make their relationship more stable again.

Having some triangulation in a family is acceptable and can be good during family interactions. Since relationships between two people can be unstable, bringing in a third person can support those who need help or are going through tough times. For example, if two children are fighting over a toy, they may want the help of their parent to resolve the conflict. This type of triangle is useful because both children want someone who will be fair to them. Healthy triangulation includes an acknowledgment that there is a conflict and an agreement to include someone who can help. When the third person joins in, everyone works together to solve the problem. Healthy triangulation can also happen when parents or other family members work together to take care of another family member, like a child.

Treacherous Triangles

Triangulation can become unhealthy in families when it causes undue stress on the third party or when it prevents rather than invites resolution of the conflict between two people.

Over many years, Curt has become a regular part of the ongoing conflicts between Joe and Doug. They are accustomed to sharing their anger and stress about each other with Curt, even though he isn't directly involved. After talking to him, they go back to fighting with even more energy. In this situation, involving Curt isn't helping resolve the issue. Instead, it complicates the conflict. Curt is feeling the effects of this unhealthy cycle, and his relationships with other family members who aren't part of the issue are suffering because of his role as referee.

Think about your family. Is there a person who plays referee or tries to mediate between family members? Is it usually helpful, or does it create more issues? There are many types of triangles. As you read, see if you recognize any of these forms of triangles.

Triangulation can be unintentional, and the individual may not realize the true impact of their behaviors. After seven years of marriage, Beth and Aafrin are stuck in a different type of triangle. Whenever disagreements arise between them, Beth turns to her mother, Joan, to discuss her frustrations. This practice has left Aafrin feeling uneasy around Joan because he believes that those conversations have cast him in a negative light. Furthermore, he perceives Joan's involvement as a hindrance to resolving marital issues with Beth. Beth contends that she has attempted unsuccessfully to communicate with Aafrin, so she seeks her mother's insights to help untangle her emotions. The problem with the triangle here is that only Beth is seeking the help of Joan. Joan and Beth are problem-solving without Aafrin. Beth's conversations with her mother are essentially replacing the emotional communication that should be happening between Beth and Aafrin to improve their marriage and make it healthier.

In some cases, triangulation is an intentional attempt to persuade a third party to take sides. Julie and Tim have been arguing about their finances lately. Instead of addressing the issues directly, Julie expresses her frustrations with their teenage daughter, Hazel. "I don't know if we'll sign you up for your travel basketball this summer. Your father never seems to understand how hard I work to manage our money. He thinks I'm spending too much and doesn't appreciate my sacrifices for this family." Julie has placed Hazel in the role of confidant, replacing communication that should be occurring between husband and wife. Julie continues to share her frustrations with Hazel, portraying herself as the victim and Tim as the "bad guy."

The next day Hazel innocently asks her father about paying for the travel league, adding, "Mom said you said she spends too much money and that I can't play with the team this summer." Tim is taken aback and defensive, feeling like he's been attacked without having a chance to address the issue directly with Julie.

By involving Hazel in the conflict, Julie is attempting not only to release her frustrations about Tim inappropriately but also to manipulate his behavior and emotions indirectly, hoping that he will feel guilty and change his actions without her having to directly confront him. Hazel becomes a pawn in their dynamic, caught in the middle of her parents' issues and feeling pressured to take sides.

In each of the above scenarios, a two-person relationship was strained, and instead of those people communicating with each other to resolve it, a third party was inappropriately brought into the relationship in an unconstructive way.

Just for fun: Identify the treacherous triangle in the first three chapters.

Avoiding Treacherous Triangles

If you find yourself caught in a triangle within your family, it's a good idea to ask yourself some questions. They can help you figure out if this triangle is going to make things better or worse for your family.

- Are both people who are part of the conflict asking you for your help?
- If you are talking only with one person, are your ideas and thoughts being shared and talked about by the pair?
- Are the pair engaged in direct and transparent communication with each other prior to, during, or after talking with you?
- Does everyone engaged in this triangular situation, including you, possess the ability to communicate candidly and convey their genuine emotions and viewpoints without inhibition?

If the answers to the above questions are yes, then the triangulation is likely to be of the normal type that necessarily occurs in families over time. The following are ways that you can address the triangles in your family.

Focus on the person talking.

If you find yourself either invited into a triangle or already in one, you can learn to counteract the negative effects. One way to do this is to focus on the person talking to you. For example, while you're visiting family, your aunt sidles next to you. She tells you how worried she is about your mother, who she believes is

211

not taking enough time to rest after her recent surgery. Instead of bringing her concerns to your mother, your aunt is managing her anxiety about your mother by involving you. A communication triangle has been initiated.

If you say, "I'm really worried too. And she's not eating properly either," you're responding to your aunt's comment with your own stress and worry. The triangle is set, and neither of you is working through your own angst or discussing it with the person who matters. Remember, triangles hinder healthy communication and problem-solving when family members resort to talking about each other instead of to each other.

If, however, you respond calmly with something like, "This is really worrying you," you are focusing your attention on your aunt's emotions. The triangle fades away when you don't agree, disagree, or offer solutions. Even though you may also be concerned about your mother and you have voiced your concerns directly to her, you trust that she is an adult who needs to manage her own life.

Step out of it.

Curt chose another way to address the triangle. Tired of being a peacemaker, he decided to step out of the middle by refusing to speak about the conflict with the involved members. He informed his brothers at a meeting one day, "It's not good for me to listen to both of you talk negatively about the other." He went on to say that he would still take their calls, but when the topic of the other person came up, he would not discuss it. He believed that he could not change a relationship that he was not in, so he gave the responsibility back to his brothers to resolve.

Like many people who don't want to deal with their own behavior, his brothers were angry with him for a while. But his boundary allowed him to feel less stress at work and with other relatives. His wife noticed the difference immediately. Curt seemed to have more energy when he returned home after work. "You even look more relaxed," she told him.

Name the triangle.

I helped sixteen-year-old Hazel find another solution. She already knew that two people speaking openly, truthfully, and directly with each other is the best way to solve problems—and her parents were avoiding that. By listening to their complaints about each other, she felt like she was taking responsibility. So when either of her parents spoke to Hazel about the other, she respectfully and simply said, "That's something you should say to Dad [or Mom] instead of me." And then she ended the conversation.

Encouraging your family members to talk to each other instead of letting their differences affect others can help you redirect the conversation.

Get outside help.

Beth and Aafrin chose yet another approach. They sought the help of a marriage counselor. They learned to take responsibility for how they felt and to remain emotionally connected to one another. Professionals like therapists and mediators will likely become triangulated but can step into the triangle with a background of training and objectivity, which allows them to help the members of the triangle return to healthy functioning.

The Dramatic Triangle

Many unhappy families have a specific type of triangle that keeps everyone in a specific role. Though the Karpman triangle, developed by Professor Stephen Karpman in 1968, isn't new, it's worth adding to this chapter because it is so pervasive, and it can be so subtle that it just seems *normal*. All three of the roles in the triangle—victim, persecutor, and rescuer—are fluid and can transform easily into one another.

The victim in Karpman's triangle is not an actual victim but rather someone feeling or acting like one, a protagonist of their own tale of woe. Nonetheless, the victim genuinely experiences a whirlwind of emotions, drowning in feelings of oppression, helplessness, and despair. Trapped in their cycle of victimhood, they are unable to make decisions, address challenges, or attain personal insight.

The persecutors are the relentless critics, the blame throwers, the architects of strict boundaries. They wield their control and authority with demands, threats, and bullying. Self-righteous persecutors yell and criticize, but they don't solve any problems or help anyone else solve problems. They usually haven't developed the skill of openly expressing their own needs.

The rescuer is the person who jumps in and says, "Let me help you!" They put a lot of effort into looking after others, often neglecting their own needs. Rescuers often become enablers, making it easy for others to keep depending on them. Because they need to be the hero, they find ways to keep others needing them.

THE DRAMATIC TRIANGLE

Persecutor
- Disparages other people's worth
- Criticizes, judges, hurts, punishes, blames
- Persecutes to feel superior

Rescuer
- Disparages other people's skills
- Takes care of people without being asked
- Is helpful to feel superior

Victim
- Feels helpless and hopeless
- Complains and rejects
- Manipulates
- Avoids responsibility

Each family member moves around the triangle, shifting roles as needed, each with its own rewards. It may feel satisfying for us to play the role of the victim, at least for a while. The attention and sympathy soothe us, and we don't need to accept responsibility for our behavior or the consequences of it.

We may feel fed up and move to a persecutor role as we let others know how frustrated we are with them. We derive a sense of power and relief when we tell others how they have failed us.

We may then go to a rescuer role, deciding to liberate others who have felt like us. We feel good about ourselves when we help, and it becomes our way of feeling significant to others.

And the cycle continues. Neurodiverse families especially become addicted to the perpetual commotion these triangles create. The continuous performances of the roles keep us engrossed, tangled up with others in unhealthy ways.

These roles act like scripts that we unconsciously follow. These scripts, however, drive family members away from genuine connections and authentic relationships. The roles develop when we are able to access only our survival mindset, satisfying our egos, maintaining our sense of security, and boosting our self-worth. At their worst, drama triangles feed into patterns of harmful secrets, unrealistic expectations, and manipulation.

Can you plot this triangle in your family? What roles do you most frequently play? What role did you play as a child? Can you identify the roles that others in your family played? Are they still playing them? By identifying these patterns and dynamics within the family, individuals can take steps to address underlying issues and work toward healthier, more functional relationships. Instead of persecuting, learn to encourage others as they grow. Instead of being a powerless victim, focus on solutions and outcomes. Instead of rescuing others, ask more questions and listen deeply, allowing them to find the answer for themselves. Stepping away from the drama triangle requires you to embrace your transformational mindset.

Kenji, who had been thinking about the drama triangles in his family, told me, "My mother asked me to talk to my siblings about a squabble they had. I realized she was asking me to play rescuer. And at first, I said yes." Kenji laughed. "It's the usual role that I played in my family." He considered whether he should step in as he continued to talk with his mother and correct course. "My mother wasn't happy when I declined. In fact, she was angry. But I don't need to take responsibility for that." Now that he can see the triangles taking shape in his family, he can sidestep many of the entrapments.

Another client, Rory, used to be easily drawn into a drama triangle. She commented, "When I'm hanging out with my friends, I hear about all their triangles. I see how they get a dopamine release from being involved in the relational turmoil. When they ask me what's going on in my life, I sound so boring. I have healthier relationships and a strong desire to stay away from any of those roles."

Different types of triangles will develop throughout families. Sheila explained, "I have four daughters, and at least once a week, one of them calls to complain about one of her sisters." Sheila has learned the art of nonreactive listening. She remains calm and focused on the caller. "I want to convey, 'I'm listening to your feelings but won't join you in your irritation with your sister.'"

You don't need to become part of a triangle to listen to another person. The key is to listen and respond to their emotions and not talk about the third person.

Unhealthy triangles shouldn't be ignored or excused. They complicate communication and amplify challenges faced by the individuals originally involved. When triangulation becomes a regular occurrence within a family, it has the potential to evolve into a harmful cycle that persists across generations. This can result in children learning that indirect communication and manipulation are acceptable ways of handling conflicts.

Effective family communication patterns promote understanding, conflict resolution, and the development of strong emotional bonds among family members. If your family is already caught up in unhealthy triangles, seeking counseling or coaching can be beneficial in breaking the cycle of triangulation and fostering more positive interactions within the family. While you cannot control your family's inclination toward forming unhealthy triangles, you can control how you respond to such situations.

18

ADHD-FUELED DISPUTES

All families have conflict. And when you are in a neurodiverse family, you have plenty of opportunities for discord. Accessing only your survival thinking, focusing on your family members' peccadilloes, diving into the emotional pool, communicating in quirky ways, listening to arguing ADHD monkeys, and creating unhealthy triangles contribute to the potential for tension. Even seemingly innocuous interactions can escalate into heated arguments. This chapter will highlight three patterns that may lead to such conflicts.

Absurd Arguments

Whether or not to purchase a bathroom scale was one of the most outlandish battles my husband and I ever waged. It all started innocently enough during a car ride when he casually said, "I'm thinking of getting a bathroom scale." That innocent remark triggered a full-blown dopamine-driven debate. The worst of our ADHD tendencies kicked in as we argued about the pros and cons of having a scale.

I went all in on my protest, first throwing shade at the accuracy of scales, adamantly declaring that they are basically the worst weight judges. Uneven flooring or inconsistent calibration can affect the readings, leading to inaccurate weight measurements. Then I argued that scales don't consider body composition. Someone might be losing fat but gaining muscle, and the scale won't reflect the positive changes in body composition. My logic was propelled by my big emotions.

My husband countered every argument, and our survival-thinking egos built trenches as we went back and forth.

"You don't even know what you're weighing! Is it muscle, fat, water, or something else? You don't know!" I finally shouted, passionately listing alternative ways one could measure progress. The battle ended in sulking silence, both of us believing we were correct.

Looking back, I cringe at the intensity of those discussions. Who cares if he wanted to weigh himself? Although that heated debate boosted our dopamine levels, it drained our emotional energy. It spoiled the sense of camaraderie we'd had earlier in the day.

An absurd argument is a discussion or debate with extreme and passionate emotion over trivial or nonsensical topics. The absurdity lies in the fact that the intensity of the argument is disproportionate to the subject matter's actual importance. But many of us with ADHD are drawn in like a bee to nectar. Our dopamine-seeking, divergent brains love to argue the ridiculous.

Have you witnessed a nonsensical argument like this in your house? Have you been a part of one? Many of my clients tell me about their absurd arguments. Some can see the humor in it, while others still cannot. The bathroom scale brawl happened over fifteen years ago, and I still believe that I'm correct, but that's not the point. I decided that I wouldn't become entrenched in arguments like this again. So last week, when my husband and I debated the hazards of polyethylene glycol (PEG) in cosmetics and food, I consciously shelved my intensity.

How to Avoid Absurd Arguments

If you find yourself heading toward an absurd argument, you can approach the situation with a sense of humor and navigate it in a way that maintains a lighthearted atmosphere. Let's say you find yourself locked in a battle about whether pineapple belongs on pizza.

1. **Embrace the absurdity.** Embrace the humor and let go of the need for a severe resolution. Recognizing the absurdity can contribute to a more enjoyable exchange. You could say, "All right, let's just admit this debate about pizza toppings is reaching levels of absurdity. Pineapple lovers, unite!"
2. **Maintain a playful tone.** Keep the tone light and playful. Avoid becoming overly serious or defensive. "I'm telling you, pineapple on pizza is a culinary masterpiece! With every bite, it's like a tropical vacation for your taste buds."
3. **Avoid personal attacks.** Stay away from personal attacks or hurtful comments. The absurdity should revolve around the topic, not the individuals involved. Keep the atmosphere friendly and enjoyable. "Hey, I may not understand your anti-pineapple stance, but I still respect your right to a pineapple-free existence. More for me!"
4. **Know when to let it go.** If it becomes apparent that your family member is not receptive to humor or the absurdity is causing discomfort, know when to let it go. Transition the conversation to a more neutral or positive topic. "Okay, maybe we're getting carried away with the pineapple conspiracy theories. Let's switch gears before the pineapples take over!"
5. **Express appreciation for humor.** Convey your appreciation for the humor and creativity involved in the absurd argument. "I have to say, this pineapple debate is the highlight of my day. Kudos for turning a pizza preference into a comedy show!"
6. **Use nonverbal cues.** Employ nonverbal cues such as laughter, smiles, and friendly gestures to convey a positive and playful demeanor. Nonverbal communication can reinforce the understanding that the argument is meant for amusement. "Pineapple debates may be silly, but they sure bring smiles to our faces!"

While we are still debating silly things like dishwasher-loading strategies, TV remote placement, or our hypothetical plans for a zombie apocalypse, my aim isn't to convert my husband to my views. These discussions are not intended to reach a meaningful resolution and usually serve as entertainment or a lighthearted way to engage with each other. They are opportunities to gain fresh insights and challenge my assumptions.

Most absurd arguments can be resolved by acknowledging that not every discussion is essential and needs a resolution. Sometimes, agreeing to disagree is the golden ticket, especially when opinions clash or further discussion won't get you anywhere. That is an important strategy to remember so you can avoid ADHD-fueled arguments.

Differing Opinions

Imagine that your eighth-grade daughter wants to ride to the beach with one of her high school friends who drives. You had already established a rule that she couldn't ride with anyone with a conditional license (under age eighteen). You made this rule after a driver education instructor showed you research on adolescents' accident reports. He suggested that all parents should consider a guideline like that. You respond to your daughter's request to go to the beach with her friend with an unequivocal "No."

At first, her eyes narrow on you, and she looks like she is trying to solve an advanced math problem. Then her face transforms into disbelief, betrayal, anger, and defiance. As she launches into her tirade, her arms flail like windmill blades in a hurricane. Her voice oscillates between high-pitched outrage and a low, dramatic growl. You are faced with the following choices:

A. Respond by screaming back at her.

B. Explain your reasons.

C. Let her disagree with you.

D. Keep a relaxed and calm presence.

If you've read chapter 13, you'll understand that option A is the equivalent of jumping into the pool with your daughter. Joining her there only escalates the situation. Adding your big emotions to her intensity will confuse the situation.

You may lean toward option B because it seems useful to explain your reasoning to her so she will understand. This won't work for a few reasons. First, your daughter is in a hyperaroused state and isn't able or willing to rationalize or problem-solve. Second, if she were slightly calmer, she would become a trial lawyer, finding the loopholes in your reasoning. "But Natalie is a really safe driver," or, "Madelyn's mother lets her ride with people under eighteen!" A long, drawn-out argument ensues, but your mind isn't changing.

In this case, C and D are the best answers. You know what you think and believe, and that's why there is a rule in place. Whether your child agrees with you is not important. You say, "I know you disagree, but it's my job to keep you safe." Although you may wish she would understand your conviction about her safety, her agreement with you is unnecessary.

Agreeing to disagree is a technique for managing differences constructively when further discussion is unproductive or when maintaining a positive relationship is a priority. As we grow in our transformational thinking, we can acknowledge that everyone has a right to their opinions and that it is natural for us to disagree sometimes. The key to this approach is disagreement with respect, empathy, and a willingness to understand the other person's perspective. While agreeing to disagree can help avoid conflicts, it should not be used to bypass essential conversations or ignore critical issues that require resolution.

Unexpected Encounters

So far we've looked at our tendency to engage absurd arguments and the need to embrace the attitude of agreeing to disagree.

ADHD-fueled arguments also may occur when a family member feels taken aback by a conversation and reacts impulsively.

After working a full day, Cami came home to work some more. She taxied her children to various activities, supervised homework, and fashioned some sort of dinner. For the most part, she managed her ADHD well that day, but she could feel her endurance and patience waning during her children's bedtime rituals. As the day's demands weighed on her shoulders, every step toward bedtime felt like a monumental effort.

In the dimly lit room, she navigated through the bedtime routine with diminishing patience. She repeated bedtime instructions and noticed that her tone had lost its gentle cadence. She glanced at her watch, silently longing for the moment when her youngest child finally drifted into sleep.

"Mom!" her son said in his quick and insistent tone that she knew too well. Unaware of her fatigue, he sat up in bed. "Mom!" he said again.

Cami knew that he was going to share a desire, an idea, a plan, a scheme, or something that would initiate an extensive conversation. She took a breath to prepare.

"I need to get some chickens," he asserted.

Cami's head swirled. He had never brought this up before. Why on earth would he want chickens? She knew that diving into his thought process tonight would end in an impassioned scuffle about the value of raising chickens. And she did not want to derail his bedtime routine.

She remembered the last time an unexpected encounter occurred. In the rush to get the entire family out the door for a soccer game, Cami's husband dropped a bombshell: he had decided to buy a motorcycle. This revelation caught Cami entirely off guard, and in a moment of regrettable impulsiveness, her emotions got the best of her. Her response was sharp and loud, dismissing the idea as absolutely ridiculous and careless. The atmosphere in the room became tense as her family, surprised by the sudden change in tone, stared at her. Recognizing her overreaction, Cami felt an immediate pang of guilt, intensifying the tension. Despite her attempts to backtrack or soften her words, the damage was already done. The family drove to the game in awkward silence, and Cami vowed that she would do her best to handle these types of surprises differently.

Unexpected conversations that catch people off guard bring their own set of challenges. The main problems include being unprepared, the possibility of becoming emotional, and the risk of misunderstanding each other. This is especially true when participants are running late, stressed, hungry, or fatigued, as in Cami's situation. When faced with a surprise conversation, expressing thoughts quickly or finding accurate information is difficult. Emotions can escalate, making remaining calm and thinking things through challenging. These interactions can become tricky, particularly when a neurodiverse individual with strong emotions initiates the conversation, deeming it urgent and insisting on an immediate resolution. For individuals to navigate such conversations effectively, it's essential to recognize when they're happening and be prepared to postpone the discussion until everyone is better equipped to handle it.

Cami's son looked at her, prepared to defend his poultry idea. Although drained from the day, Cami had rehearsed with me how to respond to situations like this. She replied, "I can't wait to hear more about that tomorrow when I pick you up from school."

Ideally, we prepare ourselves for these impromptu requests or ideas that could become disagreements. It is helpful to have these responses handy:

- "I need to give that a little bit more thought. How about we set up a time to discuss it?"
- "Here's my initial take on that. But I'd also like to discuss it more when I've had time to think about it."

- "I need more information to answer that question. How about I think about my questions and we schedule a talk?"

Be mindful of unexpected conversations in your family interactions. Hasty responses can spark needless conflicts, whether you're answering your partner, irritated with a child, surprised by a sibling's request, or thrown off by an unexpected demand from your parent. Most unplanned discussions don't need an immediate response. You can take your time, allowing everyone to focus on the conversation and ask questions.

Another factor that adds tension to families is arguing over trivial matters. Avoiding unnecessary fights can bring more peace to family life. It's essential to be patient, pick the right time for meaningful talks, and ensure the discussions have depth and meaning.

Steering clear of ADHD-fueled conflicts involves a multifaceted approach emphasizing communication and strategic decision-making. Individuals can sidestep unnecessary disputes by consciously avoiding absurd arguments and recognizing when tensions are escalating. Implementing an agree-to-disagree strategy encourages mutual respect, acknowledging that differences in perspective are natural and need not lead to conflict. Additionally, deferring unexpected conversations to more suitable times allows more relaxed minds to prevail, promoting a more constructive dialogue. Through these intentional and considerate approaches, individuals can foster understanding, minimize friction, and create environments conducive to harmonious relationships, even in the face of ADHD-related challenges.

Certain conversations demand deliberate and careful handling. The next chapter delves into applying the deliberate discussion format, offering guidance on facilitating meaningful conversations regarding crucial matters within neurodiverse families.

Ten Ways to Manage an Unexpected Encounter

When you spot an unexpected conversation that has the potential to lead to conflict, use one of these prompts:

1. "I appreciate your perspective. Let me take some time to reflect on it, and we can revisit the conversation later for a more in-depth discussion."

2. "Your point is valid, and I want to provide a well-thought-out response. Can we schedule a follow-up discussion to delve deeper into this topic?"

3. "I hadn't considered that angle. Let me ponder it a bit and gather my thoughts. How about we plan a meeting to explore this further?"

4. "I'm intrigued by your proposal, but I need a bit more time to weigh the options. Can we arrange a time to go over the details and explore potential solutions?"

5. "I value your input, and I want to give this the attention it deserves. Let's schedule a time to discuss this more thoroughly."

6. "I'm open to discussing this further, but I need to mull it over. How about we talk about it in the morning?"

7. "Interesting point. I need some time to process and gather my thoughts. Let's set a time to revisit this and dive deeper into the conversation."

8. "I hadn't anticipated this aspect. Let me take a step back and consider it more deeply. Can we arrange a time to delve into the implications?"

9. "I want to make sure I provide a thoughtful response. Let's schedule a time to talk in more detail once I've had the chance to reflect on this."

10. "I see where you're coming from. Let me take a moment to think about this, and then we can arrange a time to discuss it further."

19

DELIBERATE DISCUSSIONS

Think about how you learned to deal with disagreements when you were younger. Some of you might have seen your parents handle conflicts calmly and practically, showing you that it's okay to address issues. But for others, it might have been different. Maybe you witnessed your parents having loud and hurtful arguments, where dinner conversations turned into shouting matches. They might have called each other nasty names or brought up old problems. Or perhaps your parents didn't fight in front of you, but they would ignore each other and create a cold atmosphere in the house. Even though they didn't argue in your presence, you could still feel the tension and distance between them. In these situations, you might have developed a feeling that conflicts bring pain, rejection, or even abuse.

If you grew up seeing your parents handle disagreements in an unhealthy way, you might now feel uneasy about conflicts. So how do you deal with this discomfort? Do you try to avoid disputes altogether? Do you overthink past or future disputes in your head? Do you become defensive and aggressive when disagreements arise? How do you intuitively react to conflict? Reflecting

What did you learn about conflict from your family of origin? How does that affect how you see conflict today? What do you do when faced with someone's irritation or anger? What emotional errors (chapter 5) are you tempted to make? How do you usually engage in conflict? Do you fight back with the need to be right? Or do you give in without expressing your opinion?

Contrary to many of our experiences, disagreements don't need to be disagreeable. We can learn to address differences of opinion openly and with an even temper. Remembering to engage in disputes only when we are in transformational thinking will allow us to remain in a problem-solving approach. When we do, we can enter conflicts thoughtfully because:

- We know what we think and believe.
- We don't require others to agree with us.
- We remain emotionally connected without being pulled into someone else's big emotions.

Though it's a tall order for many of us from families who were terrible at conflict, we can learn these basic tenets and face conflict with greater intentionality and self-awareness.

on this can help you understand your patterns and learn better ways to deal with differences.

One of the most underrated life skills is how to have conflict with someone and still stay connected. *Deliberate discussions* are a method of discussing family disagreements that encourages family members to come prepared to contribute, share information, and collaborate toward a common objective. In addition to conflict resolution, deliberate discussions can be valuable in a family setting to address various vital matters, such as family values, major life decisions, estate planning, parenting strategies, and family dynamics. These discussions often involve active listening, respectful exchange of viewpoints, critical thinking, and a commitment to finding solutions or making informed decisions. When you follow the structure of deliberate discussions—(1) reflect on your thoughts and feelings, (2) invite to the conversation, (3) set ground rules, (4) state the problem, (5) explore options, and (6) decide on a solution—it can help your neurodiverse family slow down and work through issues together.

Step 1: Reflect on Your Thoughts and Feelings

As you wonder if you need a deliberate discussion with a family member, consider these questions to help you clarify what you are thinking, feeling, and observing:

- *Is one of my core values being overlooked by others?* Our values are important to us, and when we feel they are being compromised, we are frustrated or angry. Thirteen-year-old Aiden argued with his parents and resisted anything they said. When he and I worked on determining his values, he was able to see that he highly valued autonomy. He planned a deliberate discussion and learned that his parents were concerned about his inability to organize his schedule, manage his impulses, and think critically about his behavior. Ultimately, they found solutions for meeting his desire for autonomy while adequately supporting him.

- *Is this conflict due to differing perspectives, miscommunication, unmet expectations, or a combination of factors?* Clarifying what you think the source of the conflict is can provide insight into the issues related to the disagreement.

- *How do I think the other person is thinking or feeling?* Take a moment to imagine how the other person is feeling about the topic you want to discuss.

- *What is my mindset?* Are you in a survival or transformational mindset? If you dwell on your past grievances to build your case or assign blame, you may not be in a good mindset for this discussion.

228

- *Do I need someone else to help me resolve this (for example, a therapist)?* Engaging with a therapist can offer valuable insights, tools, and support to navigate the complexities of resolving personal challenges.

Step 2: Invite to the Conversation

Now that you have prepared mentally, invite the family member to talk. Say something like, "I'd like to find a time to talk about . . . When and where would be a good time?" Then add that this is an essential conversation for you and that you would like to proceed in a particular order. "Will this work for you?"

Many neurodiverse family members will become agitated. "Just tell me now!" they may insist. Some will explode with defensiveness. If this happens, remain calm and explain that you want to ensure you both have had time to think about the conversation.

Suggest a private, neutral, and quiet space where you and your family member can feel comfortable and fully engaged in the conversation. A third place—one that is neither home nor workplace—can be a neutral space without the familiar distractions of home.

Step 3: Set Ground Rules

Discuss parameters that will help you remain in a transformational, problem-solving mindset. You might say, "Thanks for agreeing to talk about this. Before we begin, can we agree on a few guidelines?" Families have found the following agreements helpful:

- *Use "I" statements.* Using "I" statements promotes ownership of everyone's perspective.
- *Give permission to tap out of a conversation if emotions run too high and someone finds themselves in the pool* (chapter 12). Everyone agrees to return to the topic when all parties are out of the pool.

- *Don't interrupt.* Because not interrupting is very difficult for some of us, we must prioritize it in deliberate discussions.
- *Don't judge.* Create a judgment-free zone where family members can express their opinions without fear of criticism or sarcasm. This encourages open dialogue.
- *Avoid blame.* Instead of assigning blame, analyze the root causes of an issue and how to address them collaboratively.
- *Remain focused on solutions.* Deliberate discussions are more effective when family members focus on finding solutions or common ground.

Begin with only one or two agreements and add more as you and your family develop your skills through deliberate discussions. The Schneiders, a family of seven, created a laminated sheet of their deliberate discussion rules. They used it when they discussed everything from family vacations to cleaning bathrooms. They also encouraged every family member to notice when the ground rules were not followed. During the conversation, anyone could say, "I see that our guideline for interruptions is not being followed."

Step 4: State the Problem

Clearly stating your issue or challenge is critical to begin a conversation. You could start with, "My feelings were hurt by . . ."

What are your core values?

How do your values drive your actions?

Do these values guide your words and actions, and if so, how?

How do you feel when you make choices in line with your identified values versus times when you don't?

What changes can you make in your life so that your choices and actions are more consistently in line with your values?

or "I feel we've had a misunderstanding." Share your viewpoint using "I" statements, and avoid blaming as you communicate your feelings, thoughts, and concerns. Then be quiet. Allow the other person to process what they heard. Will they agree with how you defined the problem? Probably not. Spend time trying to understand how they see the issue. Pay close attention to their words and emotions. If you are neurodiverse, remaining quiet during this discussion phase may feel impossible.

If you know listening is difficult, plan how to actively listen. Because it helped him listen better, Toby, who has ADHD, asked his wife if he could take notes as they talked. At first, she was suspicious and didn't like the idea, but she agreed to try it for a while. They found that taking notes slowed the conversation, made it less emotional, and ended up helping both of them process what was being said. They could identify points of agreement when they saw the words on paper. "We were saying the same thing," Toby explained, "but we couldn't see it until we were writing it down."

Step 5: Explore Options

After each person has expressed all their concerns and preferences and feels understood, it is time to consider solutions. Although there are many ways to do this, I recommend two approaches: structured answers or brainstorming.

Structured answers (see sidebar) are helpful when only two people are involved in the conversation. Toby and his wife adopted this approach because it helped Toby remain calm during the discussion.

Though you can answer the prompts verbally, Toby and his wife chose to write down their answers. "Writing helps us stay on track and helps us remember what we've already said," Toby explains. "Sometimes we go back and forth for a couple of rounds before we agree on a direction. It feels great when we finally land on something." They agreed to treat their solution like an experiment and revisit the issue if it needed adjusting.

Structured answers are helpful when only two people are involved in the conversation. The pattern goes like this:

One person proposes a solution:

"What I suggest is _____."

"It works for me because _____."

"This solution might work for you because _____."

If the other person agrees, both people move to planning.

If the other person does not agree, they respond,

"The part that does not work is _____."

"My alternative solution is _____."

"It works for me because _____."

"It might work for you because _____."

If the first person agrees, both people move to planning.

If the first person does not agree, they give a new suggestion using the first pattern.

Some families choose brainstorming, where many options are proposed, valuing all ideas regardless of their initial practicality. The Schneiders found that their children loved this portion of the discussion, and they gave everyone a piece of paper to write down as many options as they could think of. Writing down possibilities works well, especially for neurodiverse families with short-term memory issues.

Step 6: Decide on a Solution

Ask, "How should we resolve this?" or "How should we choose from our options?" Your approach will depend on factors like the nature of the decision, its urgency, its complexity, the people involved, and your preferences. Discuss how you will decide on a resolution or a course of action. Will you evaluate the pros and cons of each solution? Will you make a chart that rates feasibility, practicality, and potential outcomes? Will you prioritize a family member's momentary need? Is a win-win solution possible in this discussion? Using your divergent thinking, actively seek opportunities for compromise by blending elements from different solutions, aiming for a resolution where each party achieves partial alignment with their desires.

Toby and his wife chose to prioritize the person whom the decision affected the most. The Schneiders created a rubric to rate each of the choices based on feasibility, practicality, and other characteristics. Everyone in the family had the opportunity to use the chart to reflect their judgment.

After having a positive conversation and feeling a renewed connection with their loved ones, families often fail to delve into the specifics of their agreements. This lack of clarity regarding what was decided during the conversation often leads to new conflicts. So write down and share specific points of your solution.

Agreements: What exactly have we agreed on?

Changes: What actions or behaviors will we do differently?

Evaluation: When will we come together to assess whether our new plan is effective?

The Schneiders displayed their agreements on their hallway's corkboard. Toby and his wife sent their agreements to each other via text message.

There's not a single family across the globe that hasn't danced with conflict at least once (and some families seem to have a recurring tango with it). The essence of a thriving family life doesn't lie in avoiding conflicts altogether. Instead, it resides in the skillfulness of conflict resolution. Deliberate discussions provide a way to approach differences predictably and calmly. When we are part of a neurodiverse family, it's essential for us to foster compromise, respect differing perspectives, and strive to discover shared ground for cultivating stronger, improved relationships. Of course, there are many times when families will have unmanaged and unhealthy conflicts. Sometimes we are self-centered, cranky jerks to each other. In those cases, we need to learn to reach, repair, and reconnect.

DELIBERATE DISCUSSIONS

1. Reflect on Your Thoughts and Feelings
Is one of my core values being overlooked by others? Is this conflict due to differing per-spectives, miscommunication, unmet expec-tations, or a combination of factors?

2. Invite to the Conversation
"I'd like to find a time to talk about . . . When and where would be a good time?"

3. Set Ground Rules
"Thanks for agreeing to talk about this. Before we begin, can we agree on a few guidelines?"

4. State the Problem
Share your viewpoint using "I" statements, and avoid blaming as you communicate your feelings, thoughts, and concerns.

5. Explore Options
Will you brainstorm or try structured answers?

6. Decide on a Solution
Ask, "How should we resolve this?" or "How should we choose from our options?"

20

REACH, REPAIR, AND RECONNECT

S he owes me an apology," Maeve insisted as she told me about
a misunderstanding between her and her sister that led to a
quarrel over text messaging. "She's the one who started it."
Then, sensing that I would challenge her assumption, she quickly
added, "You can't change my mind. She's in the wrong. I have
nothing to apologize for."

How often have I heard that stubborn pridefulness from my
clients? How many times have I seen it in my family? How many
times have I had that same attitude and resisted reconnecting after
a fight? Maeve had so much to learn about what to do after a
quarrel—and perhaps we do too.

Previous chapters have discussed ways to reduce unhealthy
conflict. Still, families will inevitably experience disagreeableness,
defensiveness, and hurtful behavior because we are mere mortals
who get tired, hungry, and crabby. Sometimes those with ADHD
chase a dopamine high and provoke a fight. And sometimes we're
jerks to each other for no apparent reason. We must learn to reach,
repair, and reconnect. Restoration after harsh words is critical for

neurodiverse families because they are more vulnerable to feeling rejected, getting stuck in a hyperaroused or hypoaroused state, and reacting to negativity with their own emotional force. Without intentionally seeking to restore connection, families can end up in a vicious cycle of retribution, gathering resentments like they are badges to be collected.

It can be tempting and even feel good to remain angry or hold a grudge toward someone when they've upset you. But if you care about your relationship with that person, you will want to find a way to make amends. Reaching, repairing, and reconnecting when you or your family member is upset can significantly increase the chances of strengthening your bond with them. It builds a bridge and can lead to better understanding, increased trust, a closer connection, and more support between you and your loved one.

Maeve presented evidence that she was the only casualty in her most recent battle. Like Maeve, we often don't want to apologize to someone we've just argued with while in our survival mindset. Instead, we want to know that we were right and they were wrong. We may even prefer imagining their suffering as they realize the tragedy of their blunders and plead with us for forgiveness. As we soak in our unhealthy egocentrism, we tend to our wounds and remain indifferent to our loved one's wounds.

Not only does our ego get in the way of wanting to reconnect with those we love, but many of us also grew up in a home where reparation wasn't modeled. After a conflict, we may have watched adults continue to blame, shame, defend, flippantly apologize, demand forgiveness, or avoid any acknowledgment that a scuffle occurred.

Reflecting on Your Approach to Restoring Relationships

What is your current pattern for approaching someone you have a conflict with? When I ask my clients that question, many shrug and say, "I don't know. We just move on." How did you see restoration after conflict modeled in your family? Did you see it at all? Do you carry that pattern forward? Learning to recover from conflict is imperative to maintaining family relationships.

In my family of origin, the cost of conflict was estrangement. As a child, I eavesdropped on conversations about how family members were no longer on speaking terms with other family members. There was an air of mystery around those exiled relatives. Hearing them discuss their dissatisfaction now reminds me of how the characters in the Harry Potter books refer to the megavillain Voldemort as "He-Who-Must-Not-Be-Named" or "You-Know-Who." Although I saw this pattern as a child and was curious, I knew better than to ask. The rule was obvious: separation was the punishment for disagreements in my family. I had a family tree with many of its limbs trimmed away.

I shouldn't have been shocked when this eventually happened to me, but I was. My dad disowned me when I was in my thirties. It took many years to loosen the grip of grief, shame, and sadness. I've grieved not having him there on ordinary occasions, as I imagined him stuffing himself into a tiny desk alongside my child at Grandparents' Day, standing on the sidelines cheering as a player kicked a goal, or watching my children rip into a pile of presents at birthday parties. Almost two decades later, I sometimes register his absence at significant events in my family's life, like graduations and weddings. Occasionally, I'll read an article about a trial of a criminal and their parent who is interviewed, professing their love and support for the felon. For a moment, I think, *They found a way to remain connected with their child who committed an egregious crime.* At the same time, other parents can't get over superficial differences. But I've learned to let that thought pass like an object floating down a stream.

When someone decides to disown you, they take away any opportunity for restoration. I'm sharing my experience because many clients have similar experiences. Still, they are hesitant to talk about it. Estrangement is often cloaked in stigma and is very painful for those with ADHD who have rejection sensitivity.

You would think that because I endured the pain of alienation, I would naturally handle conflict differently. And yet, I noticed I was tempted to deal with it similarly. If I disagreed with someone, I'd place distance between us because that was the only way I knew to address differences. Eventually, I learned how to reach, repair, and reconnect because I needed to find a better way. I can't change my family history, but I have committed to recovering after a conflict with my husband and children, no matter how difficult. I decisively ended that generational curse and reminded my children, "You will never lose me. I will always love you and stick by you, even when we need to have challenging conversations."

Reach, repair, and reconnect is a simple process that you can incorporate into all your meaningful relationships.

Reach

Frequently, in neurodiverse families, children will have an ugly episode where they do and say things they later regret. Isla was one such little girl. Although she was a kind and tenderhearted child, she had emotional storms that rivaled a Category 4 hurricane. Later, after becoming aware of her destruction and consumed by her guilt and shame, she wrote letters to her parents. "I am so sorry that I acted like that. I hate myself. I am stupid." The only way her little mind understood contrition was through self-flagellation. Isla desperately needed to learn how to reach out to those she hurt so that she could begin to make amends.

Her mother taught Isla that when she felt bad after one of her cyclone fits, she could approach the people she harmed and ask if it was okay to hug them. Isla knew that offering a hug was the beginning of a reparation process. It gave her a way to show remorse without writing her self-condemning letters.

Adults also have ugly episodes where they do and say things they later regret. Initiating a reach says, "I care about you and want to reconnect."

Maeve fought the idea of reaching. She was convinced that she hadn't done anything wrong. Why should she be the one to make the first attempt at reconciliation?

We make the first reach because, despite our hurt feelings, the relationship is important to us. It takes courage, strength, and transformational thinking to be the first one to make a repair attempt.

How can you reach out to your family member after a disagreement? Some people gently place a hand on the person's shoulder, while others ask, "Is this a good time to talk about what just happened?" A good reach has two implied components in its message: (1) I want to reconnect, and (2) I'm ready to apologize or problem-solve. Please don't initiate a reach if you plan to blame, shame, defend, or demand forgiveness. Instead, work on processing your emotions about what happened.

Notice and acknowledge when your family member attempts to reach you. Try to receive the reach rather than reject it. If you're not quite ready to receive a reach, then at the very least acknowledge it. Thank your family member and explain that you need time to calm yourself. It is then up to you to come back (sooner rather than later) and make a repair attempt yourself to get the relationship back on track. Families who learn to reach notice that the next step of repairing is even more meaningful.

Maeve did none of these things. When her sister finally reached out through a text, Maeve left it unanswered for days, which deepened the chasm between them.

Many of us with ADHD find the basic tasks in life so overwhelming and challenging that we aren't always aware when our words and behaviors negatively affect others. If you suspect that your words or actions caused distress or damage, it's vital to initiate a reach and ask. Maintaining your transformational thinking as you ask will help you listen and understand when someone responds.

Repair

Christopher made a reach after not seeing his brother for four years due to a family-wide rift. "I'll be in Atlanta for work next week," he texted. "Would you want to get dinner?" When he saw the three blinking dots indicating that his brother was replying, his pulse quickened. Reaching felt like a risk to Christopher. His brother texted, "Sure. Does Wednesday work?"

Their conversation was slow and awkward at dinner as they caught each other up on their lives, work, and families. The ghost of their conflict seemed to circle the table, but neither addressed it.

On the plane home, Christopher felt relieved he had reached out to his brother. He wouldn't realize until years later, though, that their relationship would never develop the closeness he desired because neither of them ever acknowledged or worked through their initial conflict. Though they spoke on the phone every few weeks, their conversation was the kind of exchange you have with colleagues—a pleasant sharing of stories and updates. Past conflicts hovered around the conversations and were now something they couldn't seem to discuss. Christopher wished he could return to that first dinner and say, "Can we talk about what happened without assigning blame? Can we figure out how we can develop a good relationship despite our history of disagreements? I want a genuine relationship with you."

When we skip over the repair step, we risk the erosion of depth, trust, closeness, and authenticity in our relationships.

Repair is any statement or action acknowledging mistakes, apologizing when necessary, or beginning problem-solving. Though there are many ways to recover from and resolve conflict, and each situation may call for a different approach, an excellent way to start the repair process is to acknowledge the conflict. Taking the time to repair with another person provides us a profound opportunity to grow together and love more deeply.

Suppose you are the one who caused the hurt, whether intended or not. This is your opportunity to recognize your part of the conflict and express remorse. Sometimes, simply saying, "I'm sorry," is enough. Or you could say something more specific like, "I'm sorry I took my stressful day out on you," or, "I got caught up in my own feelings, and I wish I'd responded differently." Try to offer a brief explanation clarifying the thinking behind your actions. Although sincere at times, overapologizing may come across to others like you are making it about your feelings instead of theirs.

When you apologize, avoid adding a comment such as, "Well, you shouldn't have done X," which weakens your expression of regret and negates the responsibility that you claim to accept. "I'm really sorry for yelling at you," Pat says to her children, "but you know I hate having a messy house." Her conditional statement teaches her children they are to blame for her behavior. Years later, when Pat wonders why her children don't take responsibility for their actions, she may not understand how she contributed to the problem by commenting like that.

After apologizing, listen. When I spoke to Maeve about a different conflict she had, when she had blown up at her family during a weekend at her parents' home, she told me, "I said sorry! Why should I have to listen to their complaints about me?" Oh, Maeve. So many of my clients try to avoid listening to how their words or actions affect others. In many cases, I think it may be too painful for them to admit the harm they caused. Unfortunately, Maeve's unwillingness and lack of skill will deter developing deeper, more meaningful relationships.

Allowing your family members to tell you how they felt about your words or actions helps you gain empathy for their experiences and helps them express their emotions. Remember to focus on the other person's experience rather than recounting your excuses for poor behavior and defending your actions. New fights may erupt at this stage because someone uses it to add grievances or assign blame for other issues. If you see spin-offs occurring, say, "I hear your frustration about that. Can we resolve this issue first?"

Finally, in the repair phase of conflict resolution, there needs to be a discussion about how to fix the situation and stop it from happening again. If, as with Christopher, there wasn't a single offense but rather a more significant, complicated family fissure that occurred over several events, an apology could be perplexing. Christopher said in hindsight, he wished he had merely acknowledged the problem. "Simply naming that we hadn't talked because of the family conflict might have relieved the tension at the table. Instead, we pretended that it never happened." Although family reconciliation was outside their grasp, he and his brother could have agreed that a problematic situation existed and they wanted to rebuild their relationship. Honesty and clear communication play an essential role in the repair process. Family members can develop more meaningful relationships by climbing out of mutual denial.

If you are the one who felt hurt by a comment or interaction, repairs may feel risky. What if the other person disagrees that their words harmed you? What if you initiate a repair moment only to have it blow up into an even bigger argument? Unfortunately, repairs are unlikely to happen with toxic scorpions (chapter 10). Noxious skunks may not be able to spend enough time in transformational thinking to have a genuine repair conversation. A therapist or another trained professional can help you gauge whether your attempts will be helpful.

Reconnect

Even when we successfully and compassionately resolve arguments, we can still feel disconnected. "I feel like my husband and I are out of sync after a fight," Camilla says about her need to reconnect after a disagreement. "Our relationship feels fragile."

The reconnecting phase has two essential parts: closing the emotional distance that the argument caused and understanding what led to the disagreement. Many family members experience the awkward feeling of wondering how to begin again after a conflict. Closing the emotional distance is when you remind each other that you are on the same team and this is a meaningful relationship. You each let the other know that they are loved and entirely accepted.

How you emotionally reconnect depends on what works for you and your family. Isla, the stormy little girl, wanted to be reassured during the reconnecting phase, so she and her mother decided to ask one another, "Is this settled between us? Can we move on knowing that we figured some things out and still love each other?" They shortened it to "Are we good?" Camilla and her husband reconnected with physical affection. When you reconnect, you will reconstitute a sense of safety and care with your family member.

The second part of reconnecting is debriefing the event. It allows you to place the past behind you while learning from the fight or misunderstanding. The discussions usually focus on questions like, "What have we learned? How can we talk about issues before they become conflicts? Was there a buildup of tension that we missed? How did we both jump into the pool? Is there something I could have done differently?" Remember to remain in transformational thinking and focus on your part of the disagreement.

Reconnecting conversations are not about rehashing prior conflicts, including blaming, deflecting, or any other inflammatory actions. Many tell me they fall into a ditch, reviewing who said what and what was meant. During each reiteration, they are also less able to hear the other's point of view. If you find yourself in this rut while trying to reconnect, you need to take a break and return to the repair stage, or else you'll end up in a *Groundhog Day* recurring fight.

Families who are willing to work at reparation can be surprisingly resilient, able to withstand and recover from intense conflict between members. When we initiate the process of reaching, repairing, and reconnecting, we prioritize our love for the other person and our desire to have a relationship with them.

As my daughter and I sat together enjoying the last sunbeams of summer, she said, "We've had some tough times where we didn't like each other. But I think working through it made us closer."

I felt the warmth of the late summer sun on my face. I reflected on darker days when the idea of repairing and reconnecting with her seemed so far away. I remembered fearing that my family history would repeat itself with another estrangement. Although I kept reaching, it always felt like I was doing it wrong. But I kept reaching anyway. One day, we were both ready for a repair conversation. It was hard work, but we forged a stronger relationship. We had deliberate, challenging discussions and came through them wiser.

A clear reconciliation process for your family can help you all quickly return to familiar, healthy, interactive patterns. Family cultures that expect rifts and welcome repairs are the happiest. They know how to address and mend, and they have many strategies for repairing, both verbal and nonverbal. Reaching, repairing, and reconnecting are strengths we can all develop as adults, whether we witnessed the process as children or not.

21

RELATING

After celebrating Christmas one year, our neurodivergent family—our four daughters, two of their husbands and one fiancé, my husband, and me—all gathered in our basement to play a homemade version of the newlywed game. It was our way of commemorating the recent engagement. After playing a few rounds, my daughters told me the questions I wrote were lacking. I grabbed a box of conversation-starting prompts and flipped through them, looking for questions to pacify the group. After asking a few of the questions from the box, we found them so intriguing that my usually competitive family stopped playing the game, and we began answering the questions just for the sake of answering them. What followed was truly magical. We laughed, shared stories, and deepened our connections in a way that transcended all our expectations.

The moment peaked when it was my youngest daughter's turn to answer. I read the card: "Tell the group your favorite memory that you share with the person sitting on your left." Lauren looked at my husband, her stepfather, and shared a memory from when she was about five years old.

I remembered that day too. I had just returned from errands, and my husband was standing in the yard looking at our gutters.

I greeted him with a hug. We paused in the embrace momentarily, feeling the late spring sun on us. A neighbor's lawn mower droned in the distance, a reminder of weekend chores.

"Me too!" five-year-old Lauren shouted from across the yard. She ran to us, sandwiching herself between us. Now, over sixteen years later, Lauren described how she'd felt loved and safe in that moment.

When she finished sharing her memory, a hush fell over the room. My husband, daughters, and I seemed to share the same realization: even in the face of our countless emotional mistakes and the times we dragged each other into the pool, argued over peccadilloes, got caught in messy triangles, and faced deep conflicts, we were still deeply connected.

There were moments when anxiety swept through our lives like wildfire and we were in constant survival mode. However, despite the chaos, our small but persistent efforts yielded remarkable results over time. Our journey as a family had been a path of self-discovery, compassion, and personal growth. In the messy process of becoming a family, we uncovered the essential building blocks of strong, resilient, and harmonious relationships.

Creating Healthy Families Is Hard Work

In part 1, "It Begins with You," we set out to gain insight into our actions and unearth the deeper reasons behind our emotions and choices. We learned to spot those mischievous ADHD monkeys, recognize common emotional pitfalls, and become attuned to our personal window of tolerance. Perhaps most crucially, we were introduced to two powerful mindsets: survival thinking and transformational thinking. Survival thinking, we discovered, doesn't pave the way for us to become the kind of healthy, supportive family member we aspire to be. In survival mode, our focus narrows to ourselves, often leading us to point fingers and blame others when conflicts arise to make ourselves feel better.

On the other hand, embracing transformational thinking means becoming more self-aware and balanced in our relationship approach. Instead of trying to change our family members, we accept them as they are and expect them to take responsibility for their actions.

This first part of the book left you with a question: Are you creating a safe and nurturing space for those around you? Finding your healthy presence within the family dynamic is challenging, but it's the cornerstone to creating positive family experiences.

In part 2, "Ready for the Rodeo," we continued our exploration of the fundamental elements needed to create strong and healthy families. One key idea we examined is that when one family member changes their behavior or actions, it often prompts others to change. This is why we discussed the importance of reframing issues that can lead to conflicts, such as responding thoughtfully to minor problems rather than getting caught up in unnecessary disagreements.

Understanding our metaphoric entry into the pool, our actions while submerged, and our exit from it can provide valuable insights into our emotional tendencies. While it may require effort, it is possible to gradually reduce the frequency of our dives into the pool and the duration of our stays in the water. Since families frequently encounter challenges in managing their personal and collective emotions, having a set of pool rules can help to steer them in the right direction.

We also were introduced to common family patterns, like how families tend to disperse stress and anxiety among their members. Understanding the patterns and dynamics of stress within our family can help us work toward reducing ongoing tension. We also investigated the complexities of empathy and revealed the difficulties of effectively handling this intense emotional response. By understanding the intricacies of these family dynamics, we improve our ability to respond with heightened thoughtfulness and effectiveness.

Families' ability to navigate conflicts is critical. We've acquired essential tools to bolster our understanding and resilience when encountering those challenges. Identifying the triangles within our family dynamics allows us to break free from unhealthy patterns and adopt more constructive communication approaches. Engaging in deliberate discussions provides a means for discussing troublesome issues, emphasizing problem-solving and personal growth. Employing the reach, repair, and reconnect approach enables us to forge lasting connections within our family, ensuring our bonds remain strong and enduring.

Balancing Individuality and Togetherness

We've observed the delicate balance between two essential forces within families: individuality and togetherness. Healthy families are like skilled tightrope walkers, carefully managing these forces. They understand that an excess of individuality can make family members feel isolated, as if they're on separate islands. On the other hand, an overdose of togetherness can smother personal growth and creativity, transforming the family into a monotonous blob of conformity. Healthy families gracefully tread the middle ground, nurturing individuality while fostering a profound sense of togetherness.

In part 1, we explored the importance of a healthy identity and how each family member can be their emotionally healthiest self without losing sight of the family bonds. In part 2, we learned practical strategies to strengthen family connections. It takes time and effort to learn to walk that tightrope; each family needs to find their way through the different stages of life.

My family is currently in a phase of embracing new in-laws into our fold. We strive to celebrate their individuality and integrate them into our close-knit group. Together, we explore family dynamics, embrace neurodiversity, and navigate the complex interplay of emotions that shape our existence. We know that we won't always make healthy choices, and there will be times when we mess up really badly, so we try to understand and be kind to each other. Making mistakes is not the opposite of succeeding; it's part of the learning journey and part of our family life.

Creating healthier family connections is ongoing, filled with moments of grace, love, and perseverance. While you may encounter setbacks, your commitment to cultivating a family culture rooted in encouragement, kindness, and care will guide you through the challenges. Embrace the uniqueness of your family and acknowledge the strengths and challenges of it. Celebrate the moments of connection, understanding, and support. Cherish the love that binds you, and acknowledge that, like any other endeavor, family health requires dedication and effort.

Weeks after our Christmas gathering and newlywed game playing, I carefully took an old, fragile ornament off the tree. Still basking in the beautiful time we'd experienced and feeling the warmth and love from that day, I paused to look at the ornament before I wrapped it in tissue paper. Its body, made of translucent glass, was now bearing the subtle patina of age. It had been handed down from my grandmother to my aunt and now to me, and its once vibrant colors had mellowed into soft pastel hues. Holding it in my hand, I could feel the weight of my family history. This ornament had witnessed numerous Christmases, each a chapter in our unique story. I looked at the miniature work of art, a tiny time capsule from holidays long past, and thought about the generations of discord. I was also reminded of my grandmother's and my aunt's influence in my life. They had remained steadfast in their love for and support of me during my unhappy childhood.

Then I remembered that younger version of me sitting alone in the paneled station wagon in the grocery store parking lot, wishing for a happy family. "You have the family you've always wanted," I whispered to her.

No matter how our family tree is shaped, whether it resembles someone else's or features a few broken branches, we have the power to transcend our circumstances and learn to interact with our loved ones in a healthy and meaningful manner.

ACKNOWLEDGMENTS

Exploring my family of origin felt like venturing into unknown territory, but the reassurance I received from my family and friends reminded me that it is an integral part of my background and has shaped my desire to help families form durable relationships.

I thank my family for their unwavering support—your love means everything to me. A special acknowledgment to my dear husband, Tom, for diligently reading draft after draft and providing candid feedback.

I thank my excellent team at the ADHD Center of West Michigan for their interest in my projects and their patience when I don't respond to their emails.

To the Revell team—thank you for your expertise, guidance, and commitment to bringing this project to life. Special thanks to Andrea Doering, editorial director, for being a dream to work with, offering valuable feedback, and respecting my voice and intent. To Jessica English—your expertise and meticulous attention to detail have significantly enhanced the content of this book.

I am appreciative of everyone who took the time to read my manuscript. Dawn Pick Benson, a friend and talented writer, provided invaluable feedback as the book took shape. Ari Tuckman, your willingness to read and discuss chapters enriched my writing, and I am truly grateful. Sharon Saline, thank you for your encouragement and for crafting a beautiful foreword. Special thanks to others who graciously read the manuscript, including Ned Hallowell, Russ Ramsay, and Tony Rostain; your distinguished careers have undeniably influenced the content of this book.

Finally, a sincere thank-you to you, the reader. I appreciate your engagement with this book and allowing me to share my journey with you. I genuinely hope this book resonates with you, providing valuable insights, inspiration, and moments of reflection.

I want to acknowledge those of you with family histories marked by broken tree limbs that seem irreparable. Embarking on a healing journey from painful family backgrounds is profound and demanding. Identifying your emotions and being ready to confront past hurts take great courage. I hope you have found your "chosen family" to be a source of love and support.

NOTES

Chapter 1 Welcome to the Goat Rodeo

1. M. R. Mohammadi et al., "Marital Satisfaction amongst Parents of Children with Attention Deficit Hyperactivity Disorder and Normal Children," *Iranian Journal of Psychiatry* 7, no. 3 (Summer 2012): 120–25; T. Peasgood et al., "The Impact of ADHD on the Health and Well-Being of ADHD Children and Their Siblings," *European Child and Adolescent Psychiatry* 25, no. 11 (November 2016): 1217–31; A. D. Anastopoulos, J. L. Sommer, and N. K. Schatz, "ADHD and Family Functioning," *Current Attention Disorder Reports* 1 (November 2009): 167–70; J. Theule, J. Wiener, and J. M. Jenkins, "Parenting Stress in Families of Children with ADHD: A Meta-Analysis," *Journal of Emotional and Behavioral Disorders* 21, no. 1 (November 2010): 3–17.

2. T. Zayats and B. M. Neale, "Recent Advances in Understanding of Attention Deficit Hyperactivity Disorder (ADHD): How Genetics Are Shaping Our Conceptualization of This Disorder," *F1000Research* 8 (December 2019): 8; K. Blum et al., "Attention-Deficit-Hyperactivity Disorder and Reward Deficiency Syndrome," *Neuropsychiatric Disease and Treatment* 4, no. 5 (October 2008): 893–918.

3. J. S. Danforth, R. A. Barkley, and T. F. Stokes, "Observations of Parent-Child Interactions with Hyperactive Children: Research and Clinical Implications," *Clinical Psychology Review* 11, no. 6 (1991): 703–27; L. Eakin et al., "The Marital and Family Functioning of Adults with ADHD and Their Spouses," *Journal of Attention Disorders* 8 (August 2004): 1–10; Anastopoulos, Sommer, and Schatz, "ADHD and Family Functioning," 167–70.

Chapter 2 Is It You, Me, or ADHD?

1. R. A. Barkley, "Deficient Emotional Self-Regulation: A Core Component of Attention-Deficit/Hyperactivity Disorder," *Journal of ADHD and Related Disorders* 1 (2010): 5–37.

2. Rejection sensitivity is a concept introduced by psychiatrist William Dodson. For more information, see William Dodson, "New Insights into Rejection Sensitive Dysphoria," *Additude*, December 20, 2023, https://www.additudemag.com/rejection-sensitive-dysphoria-adhd-emotional-dysregulation.

3. Dr. Russell Ramsay, "Adult ADHD and Anxiety," International Conference on ADHD, Baltimore, Maryland, December 2, 2023.

4. P. A. Graziano and A. Garcia, "Attention-Deficit Hyperactivity Disorder and Children's Emotion Dysregulation: A Meta-Analysis," *Clinical Psychology Review* 46 (April 2016): 106–23.

Chapter 4 Understanding the Story of Emotions

1. Leonard Mlodinow, *Emotional: How Feelings Shape Our Thinking* (New York: Pantheon, 2022), 42.

2. Information in this chapter is informed by the following: D. Evans, *Emotion: The Science of Sentiment* (New York: Oxford University Press, 2001), 5–6; S. L. Koole, "The Psychology of Emotion Regulation: An Integrative Review," *Cognition and Emotion* 23, no. 1 (January 2009): 4–41; R. J. Holden, "People or Systems? To Blame Is Human. The Fix Is to Engineer," *Professional Safety* 54, no. 12 (December 2009): 34–41; Louis Cozolino, *The Neuroscience of Psychotherapy* (New York: Norton, 2002), 115, 130; H. A. Nasrallah, "The Unintegrated Right Cerebral Hemispheric Consciousness as Alien Intruder: A Possible Mechanism for Schneiderian Delusions in Schizophrenia," *Comprehensive Psychiatry* 26, no. 3 (May–June 1985): 273–82; Antonio Damasio, *Antonio Descartes' Error* (New York: Putnam, 1994).

Chapter 5 Everyday Emotional Missteps

1. Stacey A. Tovino, "Book Review: Hardwired Behavior: What Neuroscience Reveals about Morality," *Journal of Law and Religion* 21 (2006): 475.

2. A. Vaish, T. Grossmann, and A. Woodward, "Not All Emotions Are Created Equal: The Negativity Bias in Social-Emotional Development," *Psychology Bulletin* 134, no. 3 (May 2008): 383–403.

Chapter 6 Your Nervous System Isn't Broken

1. William Dodson, "ADHD & the Interest-Based Nervous System," *Additude*, June 29, 2023, https://www.additudemag.com/adhd-brain-chemistry-video/.

2. Adhd Videos, "This Is How You Treat ADHD Based Off Science, Dr Russell Barkley Part of 2012 Burnett Lecture," September 23, 2014, YouTube video, https://www.youtube.com/watch?v=_tpB-B8BXk0.

3. T. P. Beauchaine et al., "Sympathetic- and Parasympathetic-Linked Cardiac Function and Prediction of Externalizing Behavior, Emotion Regulation, and Prosocial Behavior among Preschoolers Treated for ADHD," *Journal of Consulting and Clinical Psychology* 81 (June 2013): 481–93; Alessio Bellato et al., "Is Autonomic Nervous System Function Atypical in Attention Deficit Hyperactivity Disorder (ADHD)? A Systematic Review of the Evidence," *Neuroscience & Biobehavioral Reviews* 108 (January 2020): 182–206; Theodore Beauchaine, Stephen Hinshaw, and Karen Pang, "Comorbidity of Attention-Deficit/Hyperactivity Disorder and Early-Onset

Conduct Disorder: Biological, Environmental, and Developmental Mechanisms," *Clinical Psychology: Science and Practice* 17 (December 2010): 327–36.

4. Dodson, "ADHD & the Interest-Based Nervous System."

5. Dan Siegel, *The Developing Mind* (New York: Guilford Press, 1999).

6. M. Zuckerman, *Sensation Seeking: Beyond the Optimal Level of Arousal* (London: Psychology Press, 2014).

7. Bellato et al., "Is Autonomic Nervous System Function Atypical," 182–206.

Chapter 8 Perils of the Telephoto Lens

1. V. van Wassenhove et al., "Distortions of Subjective Time Perception within and across Senses," *PLOS ONE* 3, no. 1 (March 2018); M. Wittmann et al., "The Neural Substrates of Subjective Time Dilation," *Frontiers in Human Neuroscience* 4 (February 2010): 1140; V. Arstila, "Time Slows Down during Accidents," *Frontiers in Psychology* 3 (June 2012): 196.

Chapter 9 Safety First

1. Brené Brown, *Rising Strong: How the Ability to Reset Transforms the Way We Live, Love, Parent, and Lead* (New York: Spiegel & Grau, 2015), 182.

2. N. Eisenberger, "The Pain of Social Disconnection: Examining the Shared Neural Underpinnings of Physical and Social Pain," *Nature Reviews Neuroscience* 13 (May 2012): 421–34. This theorizing article offers an explanation: G. MacDonald and M. R. Leary, "Why Does Social Exclusion Hurt? The Relationship between Social and Physical Pain," *Psychological Bulletin* 131, no. 2 (March 2005): 202–23.

Chapter 10 Scorpions, Skunks, and Pesky Peccadilloes

1. *Schitt's Creek*, season 2, episode 11, "The Motel Guest," directed by Jerry Ciccoritti, written by Kevin White, aired March 16, 2016, on CBC Television.

Chapter 11 Peccadilloes and Preferences

1. Ari Tuckman, personal interview with the author, July 26, 2023.

Chapter 13 Pool Rules

1. Angus Chen, "Breath-Holding in the Pool Can Spark Sudden Blackouts and Death," NPR, May 29, 2015, https://www.npr.org/sections/health-shots/2015/05/29/410331432/breath-holding-in-the-pool-can-spark-sudden-blackouts-and-death.

Chapter 14 Good Morning, Poison Squirrels

1. E. S. Nilsen et al., "Communicative Perspective-Taking Performance of Adults with ADHD Symptoms," *Journal of Attention Disorders* 17, no. 7 (2013): 589–97.

2. R. M. Alderson et al., "Attention-Deficit/Hyperactivity Disorder (ADHD) and Working Memory in Adults: A Meta-Analytic Review," *Neuropsychology* 27, no. 3 (May 2013): 287–302.

3. Maggie E. Toplak, Colleen Dockstader, and Rosemary Tannock, "Temporal Information Processing in ADHD: Findings to Date and New Methods," *Journal of Neuroscience Methods* 151, no. 1 (January 2006): 15–29.

4. A. Abraham et al., "Creative Thinking in Adolescents with Attention Deficit Hyperactivity Disorder (ADHD)," *Child Neuropsychology* 12 (April 2006): 111–23; H. A. White and P. Shah, "Creative Style and Achievement in Adults with Attention-Deficit/Hyperactivity Disorder," *Personality and Individual Differences* 50 (April 2011): 673–77.

5. Nilsen et al., "Communicative Perspective-Taking Performance," 589–97.

6. A. M. Boonstra et al., "To Act or Not to Act, That's the Problem: Primarily Inhibition Difficulties in Adult ADHD," *Neuropsychology* 24, no. 2 (2010): 209–21.

Chapter 16 Unregulated Empathy

1. Information in this chapter is informed by the following: S. A. Morelli, Matthew D. Lieberman, and Jamil Zaki, "The Emerging Study of Positive Empathy," *Social and Personal Psychology Compass* 9 (February 2015): 57–68; Sylvia A. Morelli et al., "Empathy and Well-Being Correlate with Centrality in Different Social Networks," *Proceedings of the National Academy of Sciences* 114, no. 37 (July 2017): 9843–47; Peter Kardos et al., "Empathic People Have More Friends: Empathic Abilities Predict Social Network Size, and Position in Social Networks Predicts Empathic Efforts," *Social Networks* 50 (July 2017): 1–5; E. G. Bruneau, M. Cikara, and R. Saxe, "Parochial Empathy Predicts Reduced Altruism and the Endorsement of Passive Harm," *Social Psychological and Personality Science* 8, no. 8 (November 2017): 934–42; B. L. Omdahl and C. O'Donnell, "Emotional Contagion, Empathic Concern and Communicative Responsiveness as Variables Affecting Nurses' Stress and Occupational Commitment," *Journal of Advanced Nursing* 29, no. 6 (June 1999): 1351–59.

Chapter 17 Triangles

1. "Triangles," The Bowen Center for the Study of the Family, accessed December 5, 2023, https://www.thebowencenter.org/triangles.

TAMARA ROSIER, PhD,
has been a college administrator,
a professor, a leadership con-
sultant, a high school teacher, a
business owner, and an ADHD
coach. Her multifaceted journey
has equipped her with invaluable
insights into ADHD and its impact on individuals' lives. As the

visionary founder of the ADHD Center of West Michigan, Dr.
Rosier spearheads a dedicated team comprising coaches, therapists, and speech pathologists. Together, they empower individuals, parents, and families with comprehensive understanding
and practical skills to navigate life with ADHD effectively. Dr.
Rosier's book *Your Brain's Not Broken* offers actionable strategies for addressing the profound emotional dimensions of
ADHD.

CONNECT WITH TAMARA:

ADHDCenterOfWestMichigan.com

@Dr.TamaraRosier

linkedin.com/in/tamara-rosier-phd